# GREAT
# Bowls
# OF FOOD

# GREAT
# Bowls
# OF FOOD

## Grain Bowls, Buddha Bowls, Broth Bowls, and More

## Robin Asbell

The Countryman Press
A division of W. W. Norton & Company
*Independent Publishers Since 1923*

Additional photographs:
Page vii, viii: © Elena Veselova/Shutterstock.com; x: © Narith
Thongphasuk/Shutterstock.com; xiii: © Yulia Davidovich/
Shutterstock.com; xv: © HandmadePictures/Shutterstock.com; xxi:
© GMVozd/iStockphoto.com; xxii, 2, 122, 124, 126, 127, 136, 138,
157: © Olha Afansieva/Shutterstock.com; xxvi, 1: © marekuliasz/
Shutterstock.com; 6: © anna1311/iStockphoto.com; 10, 11: © In
Green/Shutterstock.com; 14, 24: © Quanthem/Shutterstock.com;
21: © Stepanek Photography/Shutterstock.com; 30, 31, 52, 53, 76,
77, 140, 141: © CatchaSnap/Shutterstock.com; 44: © marco mayer/
Shutterstock.com; 56: © Alsellin82/iStockphoto.com; 112, 113: © AS
Food studio/Shutterstock.com; 158: © JeniFoto/Shutterstock.com

For information about permission to reproduce selections from this
book, write to Permissions, The Countryman Press,
500 Fifth Avenue, New York, NY 10110

For information about special discounts for bulk
purchases, please contact W. W. Norton Special Sales at
specialsales@wwnorton.com or 800-233-4830

Manufacturing by RR Donnelley, Shenzhen
Book design by Seton Rossini

Library of Congress Cataloging-in-Publication Data

Names: Asbell, Robin, author.
Title: Great bowls of food : grain bowls, buddha bowls, broth bowls,
and more / Robin Asbell ; photographs by David Schmit. Description:
Woodstock, VT : The Countryman Press, a division of W. W. Norton
& Company, [2016] | Includes index.Identifiers: LCCN 2015040710 |
ISBN 9781581573381 (pbk.) Subjects: LCSH: Soups. | Stews. | One-
dish meals. |
LCGFT: Cookbooks. Classification: LCC TX757 .A834 2016 |
DDC 641.82—dc23
LC record available at http://lccn.loc.gov/2015040710

The Countryman Press
www.countrymanpress.com

A division of W. W. Norton & Company, Inc.
500 Fifth Avenue, New York, NY 10110
www.wwnorton.com

10 9 8 7 6 5 4 3 2

I'd like to dedicate this book to the memory of
Larry Calhoun, who made great bowls.

# Contents

# Introduction

## LET'S CONSIDER THE BOWL

The bowl is more than just a place to put cereal. It can be a gateway to the practice of mindful eating. It can be a blank canvas for your spontaneous creativity. Or it can be a comforting cradle in which to pile your favorite flavors. It's up to you.

More and more restaurants and home cooks are serving "bowls," and diners have embraced them with gusto. If you have used the bowl to enjoy all the delicious stuff in a burrito without a tortilla, or if you have encountered a Buddha Bowl, Zen Bowl, or Gratitude Bowl at a restaurant, then you're already a part of the bowl trend.

So what *is* a bowl?

Quite simply, "a bowl" in this book starts with a grain or vegetable base, topped with a variety of components, and finishes with a sauce. Compare this, say, to a bowl of stew, where everything is cooked together; the bowl foods described in this book are composed and layered and piled on top of each other, sauced (or covered in hot broth), and served. Bowls can be hot or cold or room temperature, but they aren't tossed like a salad. Once you sit down with it, you can mix your bowl as much as you like, or you can take bites of each separate element, working your way around the bowl.

The Buddha Bowl has been part of the healthy eating zeitgeist for years, in vegetarian restaurants and at Buddhist retreats. One origin story is that Buddhist monks, who lived to embrace the spiritual over money or possessions, roamed the countryside carrying a big bowl. The community supported the monks by adding food to the bowl. The resulting medley would be the original Buddha Bowl. (For a visual metaphor, imagine that the bowl is piled high with rice and vegetables, creating a rounded shape that resembles Buddha's belly.) This macrobiotic tradition, which is rooted in a grain-based, yin-and-yang balancing practice, certainly contributes to the Buddha Bowl's ongoing appeal. Whole grains are centering, right in the middle on the continuum of yin to yang.

In the tradition of the Buddhist monks, the bowl can be a pile of motley leftovers, and the simplest way to keep hunger at bay. It can also be part of the practice of mindfulness. Americans tend to eat a bread-, pasta-, and potato-based diet, while the ancient traditions of Asian countries are more rice-based. In a world where people often eat mindlessly, you can use the preparation and eating of your food bowl as a ritual. Eating a grain- and vegetable-centered diet is incredibly healthful and diverse when you opt for whole grains and borrow the flavors of all the rice-eating cuisines.

## MINDFULLY PICK A BOWL

Your bowl is your friend. Some of the bowl ingredients like to sprawl out in a wide, pasta bowl–type dish. A bowl of this kind offers a wider surface to arrange your lovely toppings. Other recipes are for times when you want to feel comforted by the abundance of a deep bowl with its round belly.

Do you like to see everything you are going to eat in a wide expanse, or do you want to dig deep to find the mysteries that lie in the bottom of the bowl? Contemplating which bowl to use is a moment of mindfulness, as you consider the presentation of your beautiful food. A larger bowl will give you more "white space" in which to place the elements of your meal. A smaller bowl keeps you from overindulging. Some of the dessert bowl recipes are meant to be a little smaller, and so may feel more elegant in a smaller bowl.

"Negative space" is an important concept in Japanese culture and is called *Ma*. *Ma* is the calming, serene space between objects, the pause between statements that allows you to take them in, and the silence that frees you to think. We all need more *Ma* in our crowded, busy lives. Choosing a larger bowl gives you more room for *Ma*. Let your food have some space around it, so you can perceive it fully. Drizzle a little sauce on an expanse of grain, in between vegetables, or leave some open space for a feeling of stillness. Stillness is good.

Just stop for a moment to think about where your food came from, and all the people who labored over it. A person planted the seeds of every plant. Someone tended and harvested it. Many hands lifted it as it made its way from the field to your bowl. Pay attention to how you cook and compose your bowl. Give yourself the experience of making something beautiful and whole. Eat it with attention, observing the play of color and texture in your temporary work of art. Chew slowly. Take a moment to notice how your food makes you feel.

If you make your meal at a time when you really focus on what you are doing in the moment, you can find an island of calm in your busy day. Your bowl is an oasis, free from the outside world. You can put your cell phone in the other room.

If you must eat on the run, you can eat it from a jar as you ride the bus reading texts. It will still be a bowl of healthy, real food.

Main dish bowls are a lovely presentation of a balanced meal, with plenty of plants and nutritious sustenance. The layering and separation of foods with varying colors, textures, and flavors gives a bowl meal lots of variety, all in a comforting, easy format.

## DAILY PRACTICE

Your daily bowl can be as simple as a bowl of leftover grains, topped with whatever vegetables are in your fridge, some leftover beans or seeds, and a drizzle of tamari. You can customize a grain-free or low-carb base by prepping Sweet Potato "Rice," Cauliflower "Rice," or even Zucchini Dice or "Noodles." Or you can branch out with one of the recipes in this book and make a bowl with exciting flavor combinations. You can even make a dessert bowl with chocolate. (You know chocolate is a health food, right?)

On the go? You can build your bowl in a storage tub or wide-mouth mason jar and tote it with you. Most of the bowls are packable, as long as you put the sauce on the side.

Pressed for time? Cook big batches of grains on your day off. Then you can easily put together bowls all week long. Cook one grain for all your breakfasts, and cook another grain for lunches and dinners. Or prep your sweet potatoes or cauliflower. Then you are good to go. You can pick out some recipes and use your cooked grain of choice to assemble bowls quickly. You may find that the dressings and sauces in the bowl recipes become favorites that you make and keep on hand for your own bowl improvisations.

Got a freezer? Cook big batches of your favorite grains, then cool them completely. Spread the cooled grains on a sheet pan, freeze, and then scrape into a zip-top bag. You can also portion them into 1-, 2-, or 4-cup portions so that you are ready for all your bowl needs. You can defrost them in the refrigerator overnight, or on the counter for a few hours, before microwaving or steaming to reheat. Ditto for cooked sweet potato "rice" or cauliflower "rice."

Love oatmeal? Cook big batches of steel-cut oats, or any blend of porridge, and portion into half-pint or pint jars, top with frozen berries, and stash in the freezer. Take out a jar before bed and place it in the refrigerator to thaw. Microwave it in the morning for breakfast at home or toss the frozen jar in your bag and microwave it at work. Top with your favorite nuts, yogurts, cottage cheese . . . you name it.

Feeding a family? Try a bowl bar. Anytime you have a group of people eating together, you need a little flexibility to accommodate their personal tastes. A convenient solution is a bowl bar, with all the components in their own serving bowls. Everyone can compose her own meal. You can also make one big bowl food platter and let everybody scoop up a portion of your chosen combo.

All the recipes in the book make four servings, so you can mix and match dressings, sauces, toppers, and bases as you see fit. Just for two? Make a half batch. You can scale it down to one in many cases, too.

To aid in your creativity, I made the following template for you. Pick one bowl from each category for a customizable base of grains, noodles, or vegetables, topped with vegetables, beans, nuts, seeds, cheese, fish, or meat, and a sauce, dressing, or ladle of hot flavorful broth. If you want more protein, you can mix beans or nuts into the grain base, or pile your protein higher on top. If you are in need of greens, cover the bottom of the bowl with spinach or kale and let the warm grain base wilt them.

# BUILD YOUR OWN BOWLS TEMPLATE

Each of these groups of three bowls has a sauce that would be delicious on the other two, or as a medley of your choice. Go ahead. Mix and match!

Quinoa, Black Bean, and Kale Bowl with Sriracha-Apricot Dressing

Big Buddha Bowl

Cellophane Noodles, Charred Broccolini and Cauliflower, Purple Kraut, and Creamy Hemp Dressing

Teriyaki Salmon and Red Rice Bowl with Sweet Miso Dressing

Okonomiyaki Scramble–Topped Rice with Tomato and Mayo Drizzles

Japanese Soba Bowl with Hemp-Coated Tofu, Slaw, Ginger Greens, and Wasabi Cream

Roasted Vegetable Bowl with Hazelnut Gremolata

Black Rice with Chickpeas, Cucumbers, Peppers, Tomatoes, and Tzatziki Sauce

Soft Polenta with Roasted Smoky Chickpeas, Grape Tomatoes, Chard, and Creamy Basil Sauce

## HOW TO IMPROVISE A BOWL

This book is packed with recipes for bowls that you can easily build into a successful dinner. But the bowl is a perfect place to improvise, too. Every bowl is made up of a base, toppers, sauce, and garnishes. Once you get the feel for it, you can customize your own personal favorites, or create spectacular bowls from what might seem like lowly leftovers.

## PICK A BASE

Depending on your appetite, you can start with either ¾ cup or 1 cup cooked grain. Most of the meal recipes in this book call for 1 cup cooked grain per bowl. The dessert recipes are usually based on a smaller portion of grain, about ¾ cup. In cold weather, serve your grains warm, and in summer feel free to eat your bowls closer to room temperature.

## MAKE-AHEAD GRAINS

To make your bowl life easy, cook grains ahead for the week. Decide whether you want ¾ cup or 1 cup grain per serving, and how many servings you will make that week. If you plan to make eight 1-cup servings of a quinoa-based bowl, cook 3 cups dry quinoa. You'll have a little left over. While you're at it, throw on some steel-cut oats to cook: For eight 1-cup servings, cook 3 cups oats. Once the cooked grains are cooled, store them in airtight containers and use them for breakfasts throughout the week.

## RICE, GRAINS, AND MORE

Just to give you a ballpark idea of what's in your base, here is a list of some mainstay base ingredients and their nutritional info. It's easy to add them up in your head,

and to get an idea as to whether you are getting a meal that meets your protein needs. The carbs in whole grains are the complex kind that burn slowly and keep you energized for a long time—not the blood-sugar spiking sweets to be avoided.

## GRAINS

| | AMOUNT | CALORIES | CARBOHYDRATES | PROTEIN |
|---|---|---|---|---|
| Brown Rice | 1 cup cooked | 218 calories | 46 grams | 5 grams |
| Millet | 1 cup cooked | 207 calories | 41 grams | 6 grams |
| Bulgur | 1 cup cooked | 151 calories | 34 grams | 6 grams |
| Quinoa | 1 cup cooked | 222 calories | 39 grams | 8 grams |
| Buckwheat | 1 cup cooked | 155 calories | 33 grams | 6 grams |
| Wild Rice | 1 cup cooked | 166 calories | 35 grams | 7 grams |
| Whole-Wheat Spaghetti or Buckwheat Soba | 2 ounces | 195 calories | 43 grams | 8 grams |
| Whole-Wheat Couscous | 1 cup cooked | 175 calories | 37 grams | 6 grams |
| Polenta | 1 cup cooked | 205 calories | 43 grams | 4.75 grams |
| Sweet Potato "Rice" | 1 cup | 114 calories | 27 grams | 2 grams |
| Cauliflower "Rice" | 1 cup | 25 calories | 5 grams | 2 grams |
| Zucchini Dice or "Noodles" | 1 cup | 20 calories | 4 grams | 2 grams |

**Instant Fixes:** Precooked brown rice is available in foil pouches. Whole-wheat couscous is almost instant, as are some of the quicker grains, like quinoa and bulgur. Whole-grain pastas, especially thin ones like angel hair, can be very quick to prepare.

## PICK A TOPPER

Now that you have your base, you need some proteins and veggies to fill out the meal. You may find that with all the protein in beans, nuts, and seeds, you can enjoy your bowl as a meatless entrée.

### BEANS

| | AMOUNT | CALORIES | CARBOHYDRATES | PROTEIN |
|---|---|---|---|---|
| Black Beans | 1 cup | 227 calories | 41 grams | 15 grams |
| Great Northern White Beans | 1 cup | 229 calories | 55 grams | 19 grams |
| Kidney Beans | 1 cup | 215 calories | 42 grams | 13 grams |
| Chickpeas | 1 cup | 286 calories | 54 grams | 12 grams |
| Pinto Beans | 1 cup | 206 calories | 37 grams | 12 grams |
| Tofu | ¼ block (122 grams) | 178 calories | 5 grams | 15 grams |

**Instant Fixes:** Just heat some chole, chili, baked beans, canned lentil soup, hummus or refried beans, marinated baked tofu, or seasoned tempeh to top your bowl—you may not even need sauce.

## NUTS AND SEEDS

| | AMOUNT | CALORIES | CARBOHYDRATES | PROTEIN |
|---|---|---|---|---|
| Almonds | 1 ounce | 122 calories | 5 grams | 6 grams |
| Pistachios | 1 ounce | 161 calories | 8 grams | 6 grams |
| Walnuts | 1 ounce | 185 calories | 4 grams | 4 grams |
| Pumpkin Seeds | 1 ounce | 146 calories | 4 grams | 9 grams |
| Sunflower Seeds | 1 ounce | 163 calories | 7 grams | 5 grams |
| Chia Seeds | 1 ounce | 137 calories | 12 grams | 4 grams |
| Flaxseeds | 1 ounce | 150 calories | 8 grams | 5 grams |

## FISH AND MEAT

| | AMOUNT | CALORIES | CARBOHYDRATES | PROTEIN |
|---|---|---|---|---|
| Salmon | 3 ounces | 155 calories | 0 grams | 22 grams |
| Sardines | 1 3.75-ounce can | 191 calories | 0 grams | 23 grams |
| Chicken Breast | 4 ounces | 188 calories | 0 grams | 36 grams |
| Turkey Breast | 4 ounces | 156 calories | 0 grams | 32 grams |
| Seitan/Mock Duck | 3 ounces | 90 calories | 3 grams | 18 grams |

**Instant Fixes:** Canned fish are often packed in sauces or flavored oils. They are useful for a quick meal. Deli-sliced meats also make good choices, because they are easy to keep on hand. Seitan and canned mock duck are already cooked, ready to go.

## YOGURT OR CHEESE

|  | AMOUNT | CALORIES | CARBOHYDRATES | PROTEIN |
|---|---|---|---|---|
| Egg | 1 large | 71 calories | 0 grams | 6 grams |
| Plain Full-Fat Yogurt | 1 cup | 149 calories | 11 grams | 9 grams |
| Plain Fat-Free Yogurt | 1 cup | 137 calories | 19 grams | 14 grams |
| Greek Yogurt (plain, fat free) | 1 cup | 130 calories | 21 grams | 12 grams |
| Cheddar Cheese | 1 ounce | 113 calories | 0 grams | 7 grams |
| Cottage Cheese, 1% | 1 cup | 163 calories | 6 grams | 28 grams |

## PICK VEGETABLES

For the recipes in this book, 2 to 3 cups of vegetables should fill your bowl. Add more leafy greens if desired. Think seasonally. Spring combos might consist of asparagus, radishes, and baby carrots. Summertime is perfect for spinach, cucumbers, tomatoes, and anything else just picked. Fall is the time of year to savor Brussels sprouts, sweet potatoes, squash, and kale. And wintertime is a good time to use root vegetables like turnips, parsnips, and beets, which can be complemented with immune-boosting garlic and ginger.

Wisdom from the ancients can guide your choices: Look to the Japanese tradition of using color to create a bowl. A Japanese meal is not complete until it contains five colors. Using the simple idea of adding something black, white, green, red, and yellow will make it easy for you to see whether you have a balanced meal. In Western culture we say, "Eat a rainbow," which is also a color-based way to make sure you are getting enough variety in your plant selections. Don't worry about getting too complicated, just put lots of colorful vegetables on the plate and you should be doing well.

**Instant Fixes:** Don't feel like chopping? Salad bar vegetables from your local store, bagged precut veggies, and frozen vegetables are all easy ways to get veggies into your bowl.

## PICK A SAUCE

Check out the condiments section of this book to make your own. You can also flip through the recipes and lift a dressing or sauce that looks appealing and use it on whatever you want to assemble. In a pinch, you can use your favorite bottled dressings, hot sauces, and condiments.

For dressing amounts, a good rule of thumb is 2 to 4 tablespoons per bowl. For vegetable- and fruit-based sauces, think in terms of half a cup per bowl.

**Instant Fixes:** If you are crunched for time, you can grab some prepared hummus and thin its consistency down with water for a savory drizzle. You can also use salsa from a jar, store-bought spaghetti sauces, or creamy premade salad dressings.

## PICK A GARNISH

**What's missing in your bowl? Color? Crunch? Top a bowl with lots of greens. Add red chili sauce, salsa, roasted red or yellow peppers, shredded or julienned carrots, even canned water chestnuts.**

Fermented vegetables provide a delicious counterpoint to all your other bowl elements, and they contain beneficial bacteria. Tuck some kraut, kimchi, or another probiotic-rich ferment on top of your bowl—and make a healthy habit of it. Sea vegetables are another fantastic add-on, giving you a mineral-rich hit of umami (meaty flavor) and salt.

Depending on your mood, your garnish can be classic parsley sprigs or basil leaves, or a heap of slivered chiles. A dollop of sour cream or yogurt might add just the touch of creaminess to set your bowl apart. Live a little, it's just a tablespoon or two!

## FEED YOUR BOWL

Now that you have all these bowl ingredient ideas, and a template for improvising your own bowls, the sky is the limit. Pick a few recipes to make in the coming weeks and get a feel for bowl food. Take a look at the mouth-watering photographs and think about ways to arrange your bowls. Break out of your tired, old eating habits; try a new grain or a new topping every week.

# GREAT
# Bowls
# OF FOOD

Grains and
Grain Alternatives

## COOKING GRAINS

**There are several ways to cook grains. Experiment a little and find one that fits for you.**

1. Pick a heavy-bottomed pot with a tight-fitting lid. Measure the water for your grain and pour into the pot, bring to a boil, then add the grain. Bring the water back to a full boil, then reduce the heat to low and cover tightly. Keep covered for the suggested time on the package or recipe, then check to see if all the water is absorbed and the grains are tender.

2. For more flavor, you can dry-toast the grain in the pot. Put the grain in first and swirl it over medium-high heat until the grains begin to smell toasty. Take off the heat, then carefully pour in the measured liquids. Put the pot back on the heat and return to the boil. Reduce the heat to low, cover tightly, and cook for the suggested time on the package or recipe.

3. Large grains like wheat berries and farro are easier to cook pasta-style. In fact, all grains can be cooked this way. Just as if you were cooking noodles, bring a large pot of salted water to a boil, then add the grains. Cook for the suggested amount of time, and then remove a grain or two with a spoon. Test the grain: If it is tender, drain in a fine-mesh strainer. When drained, return the grain to the empty pot and cover for 5 to 10 minutes, just to let the grains finish steaming and to stabilize.

4. Use an appliance. Pressure cookers shave off 5 to 10 minutes from your cooking time, depending on the grain. If you invest in a modern pressure cooker, it will have directions for cooking most grains. Rice cookers work well for all grains, if you make a few adjustments. Use a little less water, and if you are cooking grains smaller than long grain rice, use the white rice setting. If you are cooking brown rice or anything larger, use the brown rice setting. The crockpot will take a while: Brown rice takes 3 hours on high, or 6 hours on low.

5. Whole grains can be baked. This is a good method to use if you need your stovetop for other things. Preheat the oven to 375°F and put the grains in either a baking dish with a lid or a baking pan that you can cover with foil. Bring the required liquid to a boil on the stovetop and add any salt or oil that you desire. Pour the boiling liquid over the grain and stir, then cover tightly. Bake for 30 minutes for quinoa and other smaller grains, and 1 hour for brown rice and larger grains like wheat berries. (Baking grains will take almost twice as long as on the stovetop.) Test for doneness, and if they need a little more time, just cover and put the dish back into the oven.

## WARMING THE GRAIN

The recipes in this book call for either cooking fresh grain or warming precooked grain. When you have a big stash of cooked grain, you can put your meal on the table in minutes. If you are a microwave user, you can put your grain in a bowl, cover with a paper towel, and microwave for 1 to 1½ minutes per cup. On the stovetop, put the cooked grain in a pot with a couple teaspoons of water, cover, and cook on medium heat for a couple minutes. Open, stir gently, and keep heating until the grain is warmed. You can also steam the grain by placing it in a wire-mesh colander and setting it over a pot of simmering water, with the lid placed over it as best you can.

## GRAIN COOKING CHART

Because all the recipes in this book call for 3 to 4 cups cooked grain, instructions are given in the "Larger Quantities" column to make at least 4 cups (yields vary). These grains are listed by cooking speed, so the quickest-to-prepare items come first. That way, you can base this chart on what you have time to cook.

When cooking some grains that have softer bran coats, you can vary the texture by adding more liquid. Two water measurements are occasionally listed in the chart: One is for a firm, more-intact grain; the other is for a softer, split-open grain. Some grains, like wheat berries, will not absorb extra water. These types of grains are good candidates for pasta-style cooking, in which you simply boil the sturdy berries until they are done, then drain.

| 1 CUP GRAIN | CUPS WATER | COOKING TIME | YIELD | LARGER QUANTITIES |
|---|---|---|---|---|
| Whole-Wheat Couscous | 1½ | 5 minutes (or soak 1 hour in cold water) | 2½ cups | For 4 cups: 1¾ cups couscous to 2½ plus 2 tablespoons water |
| Bulgur | 1½ | 10 minutes (or soak 2 hours in cold water) | 3 cups | For 4 cups: 2 cups bulgur to 3 cups water |
| Quinoa | 1½ | 15 minutes | 2½ cups | For about 4 cups: 2 cups quinoa to 3 cups water |
| Kañiwa | 2 | 15 minutes | 2 cups | For about 4 cups: 2 cups kañiwa to 4 cups water |
| Millet | 2–2½ | 25 minutes | 2½–3 cups | For about 4 cups: 1½ cups millet to 3 cups water |
| Buckwheat | 1½–2 | 15–20 minutes | 3–4 cups | For about 4 cups: 1½ cups buckwheat to 2¾ cups water |
| Teff | 3 | 20 minutes | 2½ cups | For about 4 cups: 1½ cups teff to 4½ cups water |

| 1 CUP GRAIN | CUPS WATER | COOKING TIME | YIELD | LARGER QUANTITIES |
|---|---|---|---|---|
| Amaranth | 2½–3 | 25 minutes | 3 cups | For about 4 cups: 1¼ cups amaranth to 3 cups plus 2 tablespoons water |
| Sorghum | 3–4 | 25–40 minutes | 3 cups | For about 4 cups: 1¼ cups sorghum to 3¾ cups water |
| Green Wheat Freekeh | 2½ | Whole: 40–45 minutes; cracked: 25–30 minutes | 3 cups | For about 4 cups: 1¼ cups freekeh to 3¾ cups water |
| Brown Rice (short grain) | 2 | 40–45 minutes | 3 cups | For about 4 cups: 1⅓ cups short grain brown rice to 2⅔ cups water |
| Brown Rice (long grain) | 1½–2 | 40–45 minutes | 2½–3 cups | For about 4 cups: 1½ cups long grain brown rice to 3 cups water |
| Black Rice and Red Rice; (for different varieties, check package directions) | 1½ (most varieties) | Himalayan red rice: 15 minutes; medium-grain black rice: 20–25 minutes | 3 cups (most varieties) | For about 4 cups: 1½ cups black or red rice to 2¼ cups water |
| Purple Sticky Rice | 2 | 35–40 minutes | 3 cups | For about 4 cups: 1½ cups purple sticky rice to 3 cups water |
| Pearled Barley | 2 | 40 minutes | 3 cups | For about 4 cups: 1⅓ cups pearled barley to 3 cups water |
| Barley (whole, hulled, hull-less), purple or black | 3 | 1 hour or more (soaking and pasta-style cooking recommended) | 3½ cups | For about 4 cups: 1¼ cups barley to 3½ cups water |
| Steel-Cut Oats (stovetop) | 4 | 30 minutes | 3 cups | For about 4 cups: 1⅓ cups steel-cut oats to 4⅓ cups water |
| Steel-Cut Oats (slow cooker, on low heat) | 4 | 4½–5 hours | 4 cups | For about 4 cups: 1⅓ cups oats to 4 cups water |
| Whole-Oat Groats | 3 | 1 hour (soaking and pasta-style cooking recommended) | 3 cups | For about 4 cups: 1⅓ cups wheat berries to 5–6 cups water |
| Whole-Wheat Berries, Farro, and Kamut | 4 | 40 minutes (soaking and pasta-style cooking recommended) | 3 cups | For about 4 cups: 1⅓ cups wheat to 5–6 cups water |
| Rye Berries | 4 | 1 hour or more (soaking and pasta-style cooking recommended) | 3 cups | For about 4 cups: 1⅓ cups rye berries to 5–6 cups water |

# Grain and Pasta Alternatives

## Cauliflower "Rice"

Cauliflower can be a stand-in for rice. It has become popular with diners who wish to avoid carbs, gluten, or both. If you are looking for a vegetable-rich way to enjoy your bowls, using cauliflower as a base is a tasty option.

Yield: about 4 cups

**1½ pounds cauliflower (about 1 medium head)**

Put on a large pot of water to boil. Cut the cauliflower into large florets and peel the stems; cut the stems into 1-inch slices.

When the water boils, drop in the cauliflower. Cook for 2 minutes, then drain. Let the cauliflower cool, then put 2 cups of the cooked florets into a food processor and pulse to make bits about the size of rice. Transfer to a large bowl. Continue processing the remaining cauliflower pieces until they are all minced.

Spread a lint-free kitchen towel on the counter and spread the cauliflower mince on it, place another towel on top and roll up tightly to dry. Unroll the towels, remove the top one, and let the cauliflower air dry until time to use.

For a less moist, more toasty result, you can also mince the cauliflower raw, then sauté the mince in olive oil or butter.

# Sweet Potato "Rice"

Using sweet potatoes is another way to use a vegetable instead of a grain. Select a color of sweet potato that will look good with your other ingredients. White sweet potatoes provide a more neutral backdrop, while deep orange or even purple sweet potatoes create a dramatic splash of color.

Yield: 4 cups

**1½ pounds sweet potatoes (4 cups cubed)**

Slice the sweet potatoes into ¼-inch-thick slices, then stack the slices and slice them in ¼-inch strips. Slice the strips into small cubes.

Place a steamer in a large pot with half an inch of water in the bottom and bring the water on high heat to a boil. Put the sweet potato cubes in the steamer and cover the pot, lowering the heat to medium to keep the steam going.

Cook for about 5 minutes, or longer if your cubes are larger. Test a piece of sweet potato by piercing with a knife. When tender, take the steamer out of the pot and place on a folded kitchen towel. Let cool slightly before serving.

# Zucchini "Noodles" or "Rice"

Zucchini is a low-carb and raw way to enjoy bowl cuisine. If you have a spiralizer or a vegetable peeler, you can sliver the zucchini into noodle shapes. For a more rice-like presentation, cut the zucchini into small cubes. Just remember, heating zucchini makes it get limp and soggy. For this reason, the zucchini must be served raw or briefly and gently warmed just before serving.

Yield: 6 cups noodles

**1 pound zucchini**
**1 pinch salt**

Wash and dry the zucchini, then either use a spiralizer or vegetable peeler to shred it into pasta-size strips, or use your knife to cut it into small, diced pieces. This can be made a couple of days ahead and stored in an airtight container. Just before serving, portion the zucchini into bowls and sprinkle with a teeny pinch of salt. Toss, top, and serve.

# Make-Ahead
# Condiments

# Chia-Hemp Gomasio

I first met gomasio at a vegetarian restaurant, where it lived in the sort of jar used for Parmesan in pizza joints. It was on the condiments table, by the tamari, nutritional yeast, and hot sauce. Restaurant devotees make a meal of their simple brown rice and vegetable side by piling on the condiments—and the gomasio is like magic dust that adds toasty sesame goodness. This variation features the traditional sesame, plus chia and hemp, which endow the condiment with protein, good fats, and nutty flavors. Once you have a jar of gomasio in the fridge, you will be able to make a bowl of grain and simple steamed veggies much more interesting.

Yield: 5 servings (about 10 tablespoons)

¼ cup sesame seeds
2 tablespoons chia seeds
2 tablespoons hemp seeds
1 tablespoon coarse salt

In a small skillet over medium-high heat, swirl the sesame seeds to toast. In a couple of minutes they will become fragrant and oily and golden brown. Transfer to a bowl to cool.

Place the sesame seeds in a spice grinder or clean coffee grinder and pulse to grind finely. Add the chia, hemp, and salt and pulse to mix and barely crack the hemp.

Transfer to a jar and refrigerate for up to 2 months.

Gomasio

# Dukkah-Spiced Nut Sprinkle

Dukkah is an Egyptian blend of spices and nuts and is usually used as a dip for bread. The incredible flavoring power of this easy-to-make condiment should not be reserved for pita breads alone, but allowed to roam free over your grain-based bowls. A spoonful or two of this potent topper can transform a plain bowl of rice into an exotic treat.

Yield: 7 servings (about 1¾ cups)

½ cup hazelnuts
½ cup pistachio nuts
¼ cup sunflower seeds
2 tablespoons coriander seeds
2 tablespoons cumin seeds
1 tablespoon black peppercorn
½ teaspoon paprika
½ teaspoon salt

Preheat the oven to 375°F. On a sheet pan, spread the hazelnuts and toast for 15 minutes. Toast the pistachios and sunflower seeds on another sheet pan for 10 minutes; transfer to a bowl or large measuring cup.

Take out the hazelnuts, then use a heavy kitchen towel to rub off the skins. Transfer to the bowl with the pistachios and sunflower seeds.

Put the coriander, cumin, and peppercorns on the sheet pan and toast for 10 minutes, then transfer to a spice grinder. Pulse to grind to a coarse powder, then scrape into a small bowl. Grind half the pistachios, sunflower seeds, and hazelnuts at a time, grinding one half powdery and the second half chunky. Transfer back to the bowl, add the paprika and salt, and mix well. This keeps for a couple of weeks, tightly covered, in the refrigerator.

# Tamari Gochujang-Glazed Nori Strips

These spicy-sweet strips are addictive.
It's easy to eat half the jar with a cold
beer. This recipe gives you a fantastic way
to enjoy the mineral-rich sheets of nori,
which are typically used to wrap sushi
rolls, as a crackly, flavor-packed topper for
your bowls.

Yield: 6 servings

2 tablespoons tamari
2 tablespoons canola oil
2 tablespoons brown rice syrup
2 tablespoons gochujang (Korean hot sauce)
1 teaspoon toasted sesame oil
6 sheets nori
1½ tablespoons chia seeds

Preheat the oven to 350°F. In a cup, stir the tamari,
canola oil, brown rice syrup, gochujang, and sesame
oil. On two sheet pans place four sheets of nori. Use
a pastry brush to paint the nori with the gochujang
mixture, sprinkle with about ½ tablespoon of the chia,
then flip the nori and paint the other side and sprinkle
with ½ tablespoon chia.

Bake for 5 minutes, then take out and turn over the
nori; bake for 4 minutes more.

The nori will shrink and become darker. It will be
flexible when you take it out, but will become crisp as
it cools.

Continue with the remaining nori, gochujang mixture,
and chia.

When the sheets cool, use kitchen scissors to slice
across the width of the sheets into ¾-inch-wide strips.
Store in an airtight container for up to a week.

# Flax, Pumpkin, and Sesame Seeds Provençal

If you like gomasio, or have ever used a spice mix or seasoned salt, then this condiment is for you. It's a nut and seed powder infused with the sunny flavors of Provence. A protein-rich base of seeds carries fragrant, flavorful herbs and lemon zest. It is a one-jar solution for enlivening a plain bowl of rice and vegetables.

Yield: 6 servings (about ¾ cup)

**½ cup pumpkin seeds**
**1 tablespoon fresh rosemary**
**¼ cup sesame seeds**
**2 tablespoons flaxseeds**
**1 teaspoon dried thyme**
**1 teaspoon fresh lemon zest**
**1 teaspoon coarse salt**

In a large skillet, spread the pumpkin seeds and rosemary, and place over medium-high heat. Shake the pan and swirl until the seeds start to pop.

Dump the pumpkin seeds into a bowl. In the same pan, toast the sesame seeds, swirling until the seeds are fragrant and popping.

Combine the pumpkin seeds, sesame seeds, flaxseeds, thyme, lemon zest, and salt in a spice grinder and pulse to a coarse grind. Transfer to a clean jar and cover tightly, refrigerate, and use on top of bowls for up to a month.

# Sweet and Savory Pecans

Want to make a bowl of oats wildly decadent? Want to make a rice and vegetable bowl more interesting Try these sweet, spicy, crunchy pecans as a topper. This topper is excellent on breakfast and dessert bowls, with some fresh fruit, or used to complement Breakfast Fruit Salsa (page 22).

Yield: 8 servings (2 cups)

**2 cups pecan halves**
**¼ cup honey**
**2 tablespoons lIght brown sugar**
**½ teaspoon ground cumin**
**½ teaspoon cayenne**
**½ teaspoon coarse salt**

Preheat the oven to 325°F. Spread parchment paper on two baking sheets with rims.

Put the pecans in a large bowl. In a medium bowl, stir the honey, brown sugar, cumin, cayenne, and salt. Pour over the pecans and mix well to coat. Spread the pecans on one of the pans, reserving the second.

Roast for 10 minutes, stir, then roast for 10 minutes longer. Take out the hot pecans and quickly transfer to the reserved pan, using a spatula to separate the nuts. Let cool.

When completely cooled, store in a tightly sealed container for up to a month.

# Coconut "Bacon"

Coconut "bacon" is a vegan work-around on the bacon front, and it's genuinely tasty enough to deserve its own fan base. It's not terribly convincing as a bacon replica, but it's so chewy, smoky, and slightly sweet that you will love showering it over a bowl.

Yield: 8 servings (about 2 cups)

**Coconut oil, for pan**
**1 tablespoon tamari soy sauce**
**1 teaspoon liquid smoke flavoring**
**1 tablespoon maple syrup**
**½ teaspoon smoked paprika**
**½ teaspoon salt**
**2 cups coconut flakes**

Preheat the oven to 300°F. Spread coconut oil on a sheet pan with a rim.

In a large bowl, combine the tamari, liquid smoke, maple syrup, smoked paprika, and salt. Stir to mix well, then add the coconut flakes and toss to coat.

Spread the flakes on the oiled sheet pan. Bake for 10 minutes, then stir, moving the flakes that are close to the edges to the center. Bake for 10 minutes longer.

The flakes will seem flexible and soft until they cool. Cool completely and then store in an airtight container for up to a month.

# Nutty Cinnamon Streusel Granola Topper

Streusel is the magical crumble that adorns pies and the occasional muffin, making them ever so irresistible. This recipe allows you to make a hybrid of both a really decadent streusel and a more healthful granola, all loose so you can put it where you want it. Redolent of cinnamon and brown sugar, this crumble makes an everyday breakfast bowl into a Sunday brunch fare; or use it on a bowl of dessert and you will be reminded of pie.

Yield: 8 servings (2 cups)

1 cup rolled oats
½ cup light brown sugar
½ cup whole almonds, coarsely chopped
¼ cup whole-wheat flour
1 tablespoon cinnamon
½ teaspoon salt
¼ cup unsalted butter, melted
½ teaspoon vanilla

Preheat the oven to 300°F. Line a rimmed sheet pan with parchment paper. In a large bowl, combine the oats, brown sugar, almonds, whole-wheat flour, cinnamon, and salt and mix well.

In a cup, stir the butter and vanilla. Drizzle the butter mixture over the oat mixture and toss to mix well.

Spread the oat mixture over the prepared pan. Bake for 20 minutes, then stir, turning the mixture so that the outer edges are moved to the center. Bake for 20 minutes longer. Cool the pan on a rack.

When completely cooled, transfer the streusel to a tightly closed container or zip-top bag. This keeps for a week in the refrigerator.

Sprinkle ¼ cup over breakfast or dessert bowls.

# Breakfast Fruit Salsa

If you add some gentle chili spice to breakfast, you can actually increase your metabolism, even before that first cup of coffee! Sweet and tangy stone fruit and peppy green kiwi make a fresh and juicy salsa, just sweet enough to charm your sleepy palate. A bowl of creamy grits or rice, fruit salsa, and a dollop of Greek yogurt or sour cream would be a dreamy way to wake up.

Yield: 4 servings (about 2 cups)

2 large plums or peaches, chopped
2 large kiwi fruit, peeled and chopped
¼ cup fresh spearmint
1 small jalapeño, seeded and chopped
1 tablespoon fresh lime juice
1 tablespoon honey
1 pinch salt
Mint sprigs

In a medium bowl, combine the plums, kiwi, spearmint, and jalapeño.

In a cup, stir the lime juice, honey, and salt. Drizzle over the fruit in the bowl and toss to coat.

Sprinkle mint sprigs on top.

This keeps for a couple of days, tightly covered, in the refrigerator.

# Kimchi Sesame Dressing

Kimchi has gone from an obscure Korean food that you could only find by visiting an Asian market to a staple that is sold at many conventional grocery stores. Part of its popularity is due to the delicious tangy, spicy, umami-rich experience it brings. The other part is the probiotic bacteria that flourish in the unpasteurized, refrigerated kimchi, just waiting to take up residence in your belly. Great taste and good health poured over a bowl of grain and veggies means you just can't lose with kimchi.

Yield: 6 servings (¾ cup)

⅓ cup kimchi, drained
¼ cup tahini
2 tablespoons kimchi juice
2 tablespoons tamari soy sauce
1 tablespoon dark sesame oil
1 teaspoon sugar
3 tablespoons vegetable stock, or more if needed

Pack the kimchi into the measuring cup, draining the juice back into the jar. Put the kimchi and tahini into a processor or blender and process until smooth. Add the kimchi juice, tamari, sesame oil, sugar, and 3 tablespoons of stock and process until smooth. If it is very thick, add a tablespoon more of stock or kimchi juice, to taste.

Transfer the mixture to a jar, cover loosely with a kitchen towel, and let stand at room temperature for a day or two to let the probiotics ferment the mixture a little.

Cover tightly and chill for up to 2 weeks.

# Easy Chipotle Pepper Sauce

True Mexican mole sauce takes hours to make, but this fast and easy sauce has much of the same charm, with way less work. I have received reports of entire batches of my pepper sauce being eaten with a spoon. That's one way to go, but I like to drizzle it over bowls of grain with native Mexican vegetables like corn, zucchini, squash, and tomatoes. Pick a protein and you have a meal.

Yield: 10 servings (1¼ cups)

2 medium chipotle peppers
½ cup pineapple juice
1 tablespoon extra-virgin olive oil
1 large onion, chopped
4 cloves garlic, sliced
1 teaspoon cumin
2 large roasted red peppers (¾ cup)
2 tablespoons tahini
1 teaspoon oregano
2 teaspoons molasses
½ ounce 70% cacao dark chocolate, melted
1 teaspoon salt

Soak the chipotles in the pineapple juice until softened. If your chipotles are very dry, warm the pineapple juice in a pan or the microwave to speed the softening. Seed and chop the chipotles and put in the blender with the pineapple juice.

In a large sauté pan, heat the olive oil over medium heat and add the onions. Sauté for 5 minutes, stirring often. Add the garlic and reduce the heat to medium-low, stirring until the garlic is softened and fragrant, about 5 minutes. Add the cumin and stir for a minute, then transfer the contents of the pan to the blender. Add the roasted peppers, tahini, oregano, molasses, melted chocolate, and salt and process to a smooth purée.

Transfer to a jar or storage tub and refrigerate for up to 2 weeks.

# Black Garlic Ginger Sauce

Black garlic, like kimchi, is a Korean food that is seeing a wave of love in the United States. It's made by holding whole garlic cloves at around 140°F for about a month or so. This simple process ferments the garlic, and it turns sweet, tangy, and, yes, black. The resulting cloves are deeply flavorful and provide a mysterious and wonderful base for this sauce. Drizzle it over any bowl where umami and Asian flavors would be appropriate.

Yield: 8 servings (½ cup)

10 cloves black garlic
2 tablespoons fresh ginger, peeled
¼ cup rice vinegar
2 tablespoons fish sauce or tamari soy sauce
¼ cup canola oil
1 tablespoon honey

Put all the ingredients in a blender and process until smooth.

Transfer to a jar and store in the refrigerator for up to a month.

# Creamy Goat Cheese and Tomato Sauce

Sometimes, you want smooth. This creamy pink sauce is a snap to make. Drizzle it over any bowl that needs a little protein and Italian flavor, thanks to the tangy flavor of chèvre (goat cheese). Pour it over a bowl of farro or barley, with veggies and beans, and you have a great meal.

Yield: 6 servings (3 cups)

1 tablespoon extra-virgin olive oil
2 cups chopped onion
2 cloves garlic, chopped
1 (15-ounce) can diced tomatoes
½ teaspoon salt
½ teaspoon red pepper flakes
4 ounces goat cheese
½ cup fresh basil leaves, slivered

In a large sauté pan, heat the olive oil over medium-high heat. Add the onions and stir until they sizzle, then reduce to medium. Cook, stirring frequently, for about 15 minutes, lowering the heat as the onions soften.

Add garlic and cook for about 5 more minutes. Add the tomatoes and their juices, salt, and pepper flakes and bring to a boil. Cook for 5 minutes.

Transfer the onion mixture to a food processor or blender and add the goat cheese. Process until smooth and well-mixed.

Transfer mixture to a pan to keep warm, or transfer to a storage container. Stir in the fresh basil.

Tightly covered, this keeps for up to a week.

# Creamy Arugula Pesto Drizzle

Basil pesto is the sweet song of summer, but arugula pesto is a perfect winter melody. Arugula is sold as salad greens, for a fraction of the cost of fresh basil, so you can enjoy its herbal, slightly nutty taste without breaking the bank. Pistachios and a bit of yogurt make this pesto creamy and substantial, and add protein and nutrients that you don't get from just using olive oil.

Yield: 10 servings (1¼ cups)

2 ounces arugula (2 cups)
¼ cup shelled pistachios
2 cloves garlic, peeled
1 ounce Parmesan cheese
½ teaspoon salt
2 tablespoons extra-virgin olive oil
½ cup yogurt, plain (not Greek)

In a food processor or high-powered blender, combine the arugula, pistachios, garlic, Parmesan, and salt. Process to a finely ground mixture.

Drizzle in the olive oil and add the yogurt, then process until smooth.

Scrape out and serve, or store in a tightly covered container for up to a week.

# Creamy Cashew Sauce

If you enjoy buttermilk dressings and cream sauces, this cashew sauce is for you. Instead of dairy, the soft white meat of the raw cashew can be puréed into a velvety, creamy delight. Vegans and cheese lovers alike will adore the richness of this savory sauce and will pour it over all sorts of bowl combos.

Yield: 6 servings (1½ cups)

1 cup raw cashews
1 clove garlic, peeled
2 tablespoons rice vinegar
1 teaspoon Dijon mustard
1 teaspoon salt
2 tablespoons nutritional yeast
½ cup water (more if needed)

Soak the cashews in cool water for at least 3 hours, or overnight. Drain the water and place the cashews and garlic in a blender. Blend to mince, scraping down as you go. Add the rice vinegar, Dijon, salt, nutritional yeast, and water and process until very smooth.

It should make a pourable sauce, but if it is very thick, add water a tablespoon at a time to thin it to the desired consistency.

Transfer to a storage container and keep for up to a week in the refrigerator.

# Breakfast Bowls

# Thai-Style Rice Bowl with Sweet Coconut Sauce and Mango

Thai purple sticky rice is a gorgeous food, deeply pigmented and naturally sweet. The stickiness is due to a balance of starches that are different from similar kinds of starches in all other rice varieties: less of the firm amyloses (firmer starch components) and more of the sticky amylopectins (starch components that gel), which produces a grain that lives up to its name. It's considered a dessert in its native land (see Sweet Purple Rice with Pineapple and Crushed Cashews on page 142,) but we can enjoy it for breakfast with meltingly soft tofu and tangy mango. This bowl is very packable.

Yield: 4 servings

1¼ cups uncooked Thai purple sticky rice
2 cups water
¾ cup coconut milk, divided
2 tablespoons crunchy peanut butter
2 tablespoons fresh lemon juice
2 tablespoons honey
⅛ teaspoon salt
1 (12-ounce) package silken tofu
2 cups shredded carrots
2 medium mangos, peeled, pitted, and sliced
¼ cup roasted, unsalted peanuts, chopped
Lemon zest curls, for garnish

Combine the rice with water and ½ cup coconut milk in a 1-quart saucepan. Bring to a boil, then lower the heat, cover tightly, and simmer for about 35–40 minutes.

In a medium bowl, combine the remaining ¼ cup coconut milk, peanut butter, lemon juice, honey, and salt and stir to mix well.

Take the tofu out of the container, pat dry, and carefully cut the tofu in ½-inch thick slices and then into cubes.

In each serving bowl place 1 cup rice, then top with ¼ each of the tofu, carrots, and mango, and then drizzle with 2 tablespoons of the peanut sauce. Top with peanuts and lemon zest. Serve.

# Sweet Multigrain Congee
# with Turmeric and Goji Berries

Have you heard about the superfoods turmeric and goji berry? Fresh turmeric has gotten much easier to find now that Americans have awakened to its brain-protecting, anti-inflammatory qualities. Goji berries are high in antioxidants, iron, and vitamins C and A, and have more protein than other fruit. Team the two with hemp to create a superfood breakfast bowl that is sure to bathe your cells in health-promoting properties as you go about your day. In this recipe, I used a packaged grain blend, but you can mix your favorite short-grain rice with millet, teff, kañiwa, or other exotics.

Yield: 4 servings

1 cup mixed grains
3 cups apple juice, divided
2 cups water
½ teaspoon cinnamon
4 slices fresh turmeric, slivered
¼ teaspoon salt
1 cup dried goji berries
12 slices dried pineapple rings, cut in wedges
1 small banana, quartered and sliced
4 tablespoons hemp seeds

Put the grains, 2 cups of the apple juice, water, cinnamon, fresh turmeric, and salt into a 2-quart pot. Bring to a boil over high heat and then reduce the heat to low. Cover tightly and simmer for about 40 minutes, depending on the grains you have mixed. They should absorb all the water and break apart; stir to encourage them to become porridgelike.

While the grain cooks, soak the goji berries in the remaining apple juice. If the pineapple is particularly dry, soak that, too. Drain any extra apple juice from the berries and stir them into the warm grain.

Serve a heaping cup of cooked grain topped with ¼ each of the goji berries, pineapple, and banana, plus a tablespoon of hemp seeds.

# Matcha Oats Island
# in a Strawberry Smoothie Moat

Matcha is the finely ground powder of steamed and dried green tea tips, enjoyed for centuries in Japanese tea ceremonies. It's also a wildly potent antioxidant and gives you a little caffeine boost. Stirred into creamy oats, matcha gives them a little tannic bite and a brilliant green color. When the green oats are floating in a moat of milkshake-creamy smoothie, you can enjoy a riot of flavors in every bite. For a fun variation, try it with another soft grain, like amaranth or millet.

Yield: 2 servings

**1 cup water**
**¼ cup steel-cut oats**
**1 teaspoon matcha powder**
**2 teaspoons honey or agave**
**2 cups frozen strawberries (8 ounces)**
**1 medium frozen banana**
**½ cup Greek yogurt**
**¼ cup milk**
**½ teaspoon vanilla**
**1 small peach, sliced, for garnish**

In a 1-quart pot, bring the water, oats, and matcha to a boil over high heat, then reduce the heat to low for about 20 minutes. When the oats are tender, and the cooking liquid thick, take off the heat and stir in the honey. Let cool.

In a blender, combine the strawberries, banana, Greek yogurt, milk, and vanilla. Process to blend. Scrape down and repeat as needed to make a thick, smooth purée.

To serve, transfer half the strawberry mixture to each of two bowls, spreading it out to the edges and leaving a deep indentation in the middle. Scoop about half a cup of the oats into the center. Garnish with peach slices and serve immediately.

# Pumpkin Spice Brown Rice with Ricotta

Why wait for November to eat pumpkin and spice? Unlike the popular pumpkin spice latte, there is nothing artificial about this version of the ubiquitous holiday flavor. Real pumpkin, creamy ricotta, and plenty of spice will make your morning bowl into a meal that tastes like pie. If you need some crunch, add some chopped apple on top.

Yield: 4 servings

3 cups cooked short grain brown rice
1 (15-ounce) container ricotta cheese, part skim milk, divided
½ cup pumpkin purée
2 tablespoons maple syrup
1 teaspoon cinnamon
1 teaspoon pumpkin pie spice
½ teaspoon vanilla
1 pinch salt
½ cup dried cranberries, chopped
½ cup walnuts, chopped
1 tablespoon sugar mixed with 1 teaspoon ground cinnamon, optional

Warm up cooked rice.

In a food processor, purée 1 cup of the ricotta, then add the pumpkin, maple syrup, cinnamon, pie spice, vanilla, and salt and process until smooth.

Stir the pumpkin mixture into the warm brown rice.

Serve 1 cup of pumpkin brown rice in each bowl, topped with cranberries, walnuts, and about 3 tablespoons of the remaining ricotta. Sprinkle with cinnamon sugar, if desired.

# Multigrain Polenta with Pesto Eggs and Kale

Make the polenta on Sunday, and you can enjoy it all week long. A quick scramble of pesto-laced eggs and some seared vegetables will get your day off to a seriously well-fed start. The polenta can be a great swap for grains in other bowls too, and these toppings work just as well with amaranth or teff.

Yield: 4 servings

2 tablespoons plus 1 teaspoon unsalted
    butter, divided
¾ cup cornmeal, coarse
¼ cup buckwheat groats
¼ cup millet
3½ cups water
1 teaspoon salt
½ cup shredded Parmesan cheese
1 cup fresh parsley
1 clove garlic
2 tablespoons pine nuts
¼ teaspoon salt
1 tablespoon extra-virgin olive oil
8 large eggs
Olive oil, for pan
1 large carrot, sliced
1 bunch kale, stems removed, chopped

For the polenta, butter a loaf pan with a teaspoon of the butter and reserve. Combine the cornmeal, buckwheat, and millet in a 2-quart saucepan and whisk in the water and salt. Place over medium-high heat to bring to a boil, then reduce the heat to low or medium-low and stir, scraping the bottom of the pan, every 5 minutes. Cook until very thick, about 30 minutes. Stir in remaining butter and Parmesan. Scrape into the prepared loaf pan and smooth the top. Let cool, and chill until firm, if desired.

For the pesto, place the parsley, garlic, pine nuts, and salt in a food processor and process to a coarse grind. Scrape down and add the olive oil, and process until a paste is formed. Crack the eggs into a large bowl and whisk, then whisk in the pesto.

Slice the polenta into 12 slices and place them carefully on a plate to microwave, or you can sear them in a sauté pan. In a large sauté pan, smear a dab of olive oil and quickly sauté the carrot for a couple of minutes, remove to a plate, then sauté the kale for a couple of minutes and remove. Smear in a little more oil and scramble the eggs over medium heat.

Serve warmed polenta slices in four bowls, topped with ¼ each of the carrots, kale, and eggs. Serve immediately.

# Savory Porridge with Grilled Sausages, Scrambled Eggs, and Steamed Kale

Start your day with the breakfast of a farmhand, updated to include grains and greens. Veg-heads can sub their favorite nonmeat sausages, and tofu easily scrambles up in place of eggs. You can cook the eggs however you want: scrambled, over easy, whatever works for you in the morning. Get a variation going by using another grain like freekeh, bulgur, or even boiled barley to make a ploughman's breakfast that sticks to your ribs.

Yield: 4 servings

3 cups water
1 cup steel-cut oats
1 large carrot, quartered and sliced
¼ teaspoon salt
½ cup shredded Parmesan cheese, divided
1 bunch kale, stemmed and chopped
4 (4 ounces) sausage links
4 large eggs

Bring the water, steel-cut oats, carrot, and salt to a boil in a 4-quart pot, and then lower to a simmer. Stir every 10 minutes for 30 minutes or so. Take off the heat and stir in half the Parmesan cheese. Cover and let stand until serving.

Set up a steamer and steam the kale for 2 minutes. Meanwhile, fry the sausage links in a large skillet, turning to brown evenly for about 5 minutes, depending on their size, and once cooked, transfer the meat to a plate. Cook the eggs in the same fat as the sausage, either scrambled or sunny side up. Serve 1 cup of oats in each bowl; top with kale, sausage, and an egg, and sprinkle with the remaining Parmesan.

# Sweet Potatoes
# with Curried Eggs and Spinach

Start your day with a kick, and you will dance through your busy morning. A base of sweet potatoes provides a tender, sweet spot to nestle some eggs (or tofu) alongside spinach and tomatoes.

Yield: 4 servings

**1½ pounds sweet potatoes (4 cups cubed)**
**¾ cup coconut milk**
**1 teaspoon curry powder**
**½ teaspoon salt**
**8 cups baby spinach, chopped**
**8 large eggs or 1 (10-ounce) package firm tofu, cubed**
**2 small tomatoes, chopped**

Slice the sweet potatoes into ¼-inch-thick slices, then stack the slices and slice them into ¼-inch strips. Slice the strips into small cubes.

Place a steamer into a large pot with half an inch water in the bottom and bring the water to a boil. Put the sweet potato cubes in the steamer and cover the pot, lowering the heat to medium to keep the steam going. Cook for about 5 minutes, or longer if your cubes are larger. Test a piece of sweet potato by piercing with a knife. When tender, take the steamer out of the pot and place on a folded kitchen towel.

For the topping, warm the coconut milk in a large skillet. Add the curry powder and salt and stir; raise the heat to medium-high and stir in the spinach. Turn the spinach to coat, and cook just until it starts to wilt, then transfer to a bowl. Crack the eggs into the pan, and cover the pan with a lid. (If using tofu, add it to the pan and stir, and simmer until thick, about 5 minutes.)

Check eggs every two minutes, shaking the pan a little to see if the whites are becoming firm. Turn off the heat when the eggs are done to your liking.

To serve, portion a cup of sweet potato into each bowl, then place two eggs and ¼ of the spinach mixture on top. Top with tomatoes and serve.

# Deluxe Oat Bowl with Berries, Cottage Cheese, Shredded Carrots, and Granola

You can also try this recipe with whole oats, or jazz it up even more with the Nutty Cinnamon Streusel Granola Topper (page 20). Either way, you'll forget that you are fueling up with lots of fiber and protein—it's so delicious that you won't even care that it's good for you. Even better, this breakfast bowl packs into a jar for easy toting. Bonus points for swapping in blackberries or mulberries, if you can get them!

Yield: 4 servings

4 cups cooked steel-cut oats or whole-oat groats
1 pinch salt
2 cups shredded carrots
1 teaspoon cinnamon
1 teaspoon honey
2 cups cottage cheese
12 ounces (2 cups) fresh raspberries
1 cup granola

Warm the oats and add pinch of salt. In a medium bowl, stir the carrots with cinnamon and honey.

In each bowl, serve 1 cup oats topped with carrots, cottage cheese, and raspberries, then sprinkle with ¼ of the granola.

This also can be assembled in four wide-mouth quart jars for ease of transport.

# Greek Barley with Dates, Walnuts, and Spice with Greek Yogurt

Greeks and barley go way back, so why not celebrate their long-term relationship with a tasty breakfast bowl? Savory rosemary and walnuts meet sweet dates and honey in a lively Mediterranean romance. Currants are the dried version of ancient Corinthian grapes, which originated on the island of Zante.

Yield: 4 servings

2½ cups water
1 cup barley, pearled or hulled
1 tablespoon fresh rosemary
1 tablespoon extra-virgin olive oil
1 teaspoon cinnamon
2 tablespoons lemon juice, plus 1 tablespoon zest
3 tablespoons honey, divided
1 cup dates, pitted and sliced
1 cup walnut halves
2 cups Greek yogurt, plain
1 scallion, slivered, optional
½ cup dried currants or goji berries, optional

In a 1-quart pot, bring the water to a boil. Add the barley, rosemary, and olive oil and return to boil. Cover, reduce the heat to low, and cook for about 30 minutes for pearled barley, or up to 50 minutes for hulled barley. Take off the heat when tender, drain if necessary.

In a small cup, stir the cinnamon, lemon, and 1 tablespoon of the honey, then drizzle over the cooked barley. Toss to mix.

Serve ¼ of the barley in each bowl. On top of each, arrange dates, walnuts, half a cup of Greek yogurt, and a drizzle of the remaining honey. Top with lemon zest, and, if using, scallions, currants, or goji berries and serve.

# Orange-Oat Tabouli with Parsley, Pistachios, and Carrots

Regular tabouli has been done to death in certain circles. Time to branch out and use the form for a fruity breakfast. This sprightly cold breakfast is easy to make ahead, so you can grab it out of the refrigerator and bowl up your morning. For an extra special dish, try it with Cara Cara oranges or even blood oranges, when these exotic citrus hit the markets.

Yield: 4 servings

3 cups cooked freekeh or oat groats
1½ cups shredded carrots
2 large oranges, divided
3 tablespoons extra-virgin olive oil
3 tablespoons honey
1 tablespoon lemon juice
1½ cups fresh parsley, chopped
1 cup shelled pistachios, chopped

Warm the grains. Stir in the shredded carrots and let cool. Zest one orange to make 2 teaspoons zest and stir the zest into the grains.

Juice one orange to make ¼ cup juice, and stir in the olive oil, honey, and lemon juice. Pour over the cooled grain. Stir in the parsley.

Peel the remaining orange and chop the sections into small bite-size pieces. Serve ¾ cup of the grain mixture topped with orange pieces and pistachios.

# Picky Kid's Brown Rice with Peaches and Peanut Butter-Honey Topping

I have to admit, I got this idea from a mom who came to one of my cooking classes. Her version was just peanut butter, honey, and brown rice. I dolled it up just a touch. Still, you can pull this together in minutes, and even kids who turn up their noses at healthy meals will dig in. Don't be embarrassed if you love it, too.

Yield: 4 servings

4 cups cooked brown rice or other grain
2 cups shredded carrots
2 (14.5-ounce) cans sliced peaches, no sugar added (save the juice)
½ cup peanut butter, unsweetened
2 tablespoons honey
½ teaspoon salt
2 cups red grapes
½ cup chopped peanuts

Warm the rice, then stir in the carrots.

Drain the peaches, reserving the juice in a cup. In a small bowl, stir the peanut butter, honey, ½ cup of the peach juice, and salt. Stir the peanut sauce into the brown rice.

Serve about ¾ cup per bowl. Top with peaches and grapes and sprinkle with peanuts.

# Matcha Tea Rice with Sliced Melon, Pickled Ginger, and Lox

I'm pretty sure that the Japanese don't mix matcha in their rice, but boy howdy, is it *oishii* (delicious!). Melon and cured fish give this bowl a Japanese feel, and the lush melon also cleanses the palate between bites. This one refreshes as it fuels you for a serious day of contemplation and movement. This packs well.

Yield: 4 servings

3 teaspoons matcha
4 cups cooked long- or short-grain brown rice
¼ cup sliced pickled ginger
1 (2½ pound) cantaloupe, peeled, seeded, and sliced
8 ounces lox, slivered
4 teaspoons black sesame seeds
½ cup plain yogurt (not Greek)

Stir the matcha into the cooked rice.

To serve, divide the brown rice between the bowls. Arrange ¼ of the pickled ginger in each bowl. Arrange the slices of cantaloupe around half of each bowl. Mound the lox on the opposite side. Sprinkle the lox with black sesame, and then dollop stirred yogurt over the cantaloupe. Serve.

# Pomegranate Couscous with Hemp, Chia, Raspberries, and Pear

Whole-grain couscous is instant "grain" made with whole-wheat flour. It's not quite as wholesome as a bowl of wheat berries, but it sure cooks more quickly. I love this bowl because the little couscous grains absorb the bright red pomegranate juice, making a purplish, soft base for juicy berries and crunchy Asian pears and seeds.

Yield: 4 servings

1 cup water
1¼ cups pomegranate juice
1½ cups whole-wheat couscous
1 large Asian pear, sliced
2 cups (12 ounces) fresh raspberries
¼ cup hemp seeds
¼ cup chia seeds

In a 1-quart pot, combine the water and juice, and bring to a boil over high heat. Stir in the couscous and cover, then take off the heat. Let stand for 5 minutes.

Serve ¾ cup couscous in each bowl, then arrange the Asian pear slices around the edges. Sprinkle with raspberries, then hemp and chia seeds. Serve warm.

Lunch Bowls

# Black Rice, Tofu, and Greens Bowl with Kimchi and Spicy Mayo

Keep it simple and get your fermented cabbage in for the day, boosting your good bacteria. This bowl is so macrobiotic and plant-based that it gives you instant karma points. Pack it and take to work, but wait to add the nori 'til the last minute. Bonus points for sprinkling this bowl with Chia-Hemp Gomasio (page 12).

Yield: 4 servings

1 (14-ounce) package firm tofu
2 teaspoons canola oil
2 tablespoons tamari soy sauce, plus extra to pass
2 tablespoons honey
4 cups cooked black rice
3 tablespoons rice vinegar, divided
1 teaspoon sugar
½ cup mayonnaise
2 tablespoons gochujang (Korean hot sauce)
1 bunch kale, shredded
1 cup kimchi, drained
4 large radishes, thinly sliced

Preheat the oven to 400°F. Drain the tofu, wrap in a towel, and press gently to remove excess water. Slice the pressed tofu across the short side to make 8 slices. Spread the canola oil on a sheet pan and place the tofu on the pan. Stir the tamari and the honey in a cup, then spread the tamari mixture evenly on the tofu pieces. Bake for 20 minutes, then use a spatula to turn the slices and bake for 20 minutes longer. Let cool.

Warm the black rice. Mix 1 tablespoon of the rice vinegar and sugar and fold it gently into the rice.

Stir the mayonnaise, remaining rice vinegar, and gochujang in a cup.

To serve, divide the rice between the bowls, then arrange the baked tofu, kale, kimchi, and radishes on top. Drizzle ¼ of the mayo dressing on top of each. Serve with tamari on the side.

# Salmon Bowl with Quinoa, Cabbage, Apple, and Caraway Yogurt Dressing

This one borrows flavors from Northern Europe, with lox, caraway, cabbage, and apples in a tangy yogurt sauce. The flavorful topping complements the nutty taste of quinoa. Or you could try it with another favorite grain such as buckwheat or barley.

Yield: 4 servings

2 tablespoons extra-virgin olive oil, divided
¼ cup chopped shallot
1 teaspoon caraway seeds
½ cup plain yogurt (not Greek)
1 tablespoon Dijon mustard
1 teaspoon sugar
½ teaspoon salt
2 cups red cabbage, thinly sliced
2 large apples, thinly sliced
4 cups cooked quinoa
8 ounces lox

Warm the quinoa.

In a small pot, heat half the olive oil and sauté the shallots and caraway seeds. When the shallots are softened, about 4 minutes, take off the heat. Let cool for a few minutes, then stir in the yogurt, Dijon, sugar, and salt. Reserve dressing.

In a medium skillet, heat the remaining oil and sauté the cabbage for about 5 minutes; transfer to a plate. Sauté the apples until browned and softened, about 4 minutes.

Serve the quinoa in bowls, topped with cabbage, apples, lox, and dressing.

# Thai Tuna Salad Bowl with Sweet Pickles and Lime-Chili Dressing

If you think tuna salad always involves mayonnaise, prepare to have your mind blown! Canned tuna, or salmon if you prefer, is the perfect match for a light, bright lime and chili dressing. Tangy, meaty, chewy, and spiked with crunchy sweet pickles, this will wake up your palate and fuel you through a productive afternoon. This is a good lunchbox bowl— just toss it when you're ready.

Yield: 4 servings

¼ cup fresh lime juice
2 tablespoons sugar
2 tablespoons soy sauce
1 medium red jalapeño, seeded and chopped
4 (5-ounce) cans tuna in oil (save the juices)
2 medium scallions, chopped and divided
4 cups cooked brown rice
2 cups finely shredded cabbage
12 small sweet pickles
¼ cup cilantro leaves, torn

First, make the dressing. In a cup, stir the lime juice, sugar, soy sauce, and red jalapeño. Reserve 2 tablespoons of the tuna liquid and drain the tuna. Incorporate the liquid into the dressing and stir.

Put the tuna in a medium bowl and break it up, if needed, and drizzle with ¼ cup of the dressing. Add half the scallions, and toss to mix.

In each bowl, place ¼ of the rice, drizzle with remaining dressing, and arrange the prepared tuna, cabbage, and sweet pickles on top. Garnish with the remaining scallions and cilantro leaves. Serve.

# Buckwheat and Seared Cabbage with Braised Squash Chunks and Smoked Almonds

Buckwheat is part of the Russian and Northern European food pantheon and is often paired with cabbage. The nutty, earthy taste of the buckwheat is perfect with tender squash. A little apple juice adds a tangy sweetness. Smoked almonds add crunch, umami, and protein, so dig in.

Yield: 4 servings

**4 cups cooked buckwheat groats**
**1 tablespoon extra-virgin olive oil, divided**
**3 cups winter squash, peeled and cubed**
**½ cup chopped onion**
**½ cup apple juice**
**1 teaspoon salt, divided**
**3 cups shredded red and green cabbage**
**2 cloves garlic, chopped**
**¾ cup smoked almonds, coarsely chopped**

Warm the buckwheat.

In a medium sauté pan with a lid, heat 2 teaspoons of the olive oil and add the squash and onion. Sauté over medium-high heat for 4 minutes to soften the onions and brown the squash a little. Add the apple juice to the pan, quickly cover it, and reduce the heat to medium-low. Cook for about 7 minutes, depending on the size of the squash cubes. Take the lid off and test by piercing a cube with a paring knife; the tip should slip in easily. Season with half a teaspoon of the salt and stir until the liquids are dry. Transfer the squash to a bowl and keep warm.

Add the remaining teaspoon of olive oil to the pan and place over medium-high heat. Add the cabbage and cook, stirring, until the leaves are lightly browned and softened, about 4 minutes. Add the garlic and stir for just a minute more. Season with remaining salt.

Serve ¼ of the buckwheat in each bowl, topped with squash, cabbage, and smoked almonds.

# Quinoa, Black Bean, and Kale Bowl with Sriracha-Apricot Dressing

Make extra of this dressing; it is really just that good. Sweet, sour, fruity, spicy, this pourable elixir will fix up any bowl that needs a little kick. It can even bring to life a boring burrito or salad. This is a quintessential bowl, loaded up with beans and veggies, and sure to satisfy and delight with every bite.

Yield: 4 servings

4 cups cooked quinoa
¼ cup apricot jam
¼ cup tamari soy sauce
2 tablespoons sriracha sauce
2 tablespoons cider vinegar
1 clove garlic, pressed
2 cups cooked black beans, rinsed and drained
4 ounces baby kale, chopped
1 cup pickled beets, slivered
1 cup shredded carrot
1 cup microgreens, washed and dried

Warm the quinoa.

In a medium bowl or Pyrex cup, stir the jam, tamari, sriracha, cider vinegar, and garlic. Reserve.

In each of four wide pasta bowls, place ¼ of the quinoa, and arrange equally the beans and all the remaining ingredients on top. Drizzle with dressing and serve.

# Easier Bibimbap with Brown Rice, Tofu or Eggs, Sautéed Shiitakes, Kimchi, and Spiced Nori

Bibimbap is the Korean rice bowl that is closest to sushi in its components, except much spicier and more casual. Traditionally, it's a bowl of rice supported by lots of smaller bowls of *banchan* that consist of tasty pickles, vegetables, and toppings that diners add to their rice as they eat. This is a much more abbreviated version, so you can revel in the amazing flavors without making all the *banchan*. You can use prebaked tofu for this, or make the tofu as described in the recipe for Black Rice, Tofu, and Greens Bowl with Kimchi and Spicy Mayo (page 54).

Yield: 4 servings

4 cups cooked short-grain brown rice
1 medium cucumber, peeled, seeded, and sliced
1 tablespoon rice vinegar
1 tablespoon sugar
1 pinch salt
2 teaspoons canola oil, divided
8 ounces fresh shiitakes, caps slivered
2 tablespoons mirin
3 teaspoons tamari soy sauce, divided
2 teaspoons rice vinegar, divided
8 ounces salad spinach
6 cloves black garlic, sliced
2 large carrots, julienned
1 pound baked tofu or 4 eggs
½ cup kimchi
1 sheet seasoned nori, sliced in strips
Gochujang (Korean hot sauce), to serve

Warm the rice. If desired, start with cold rice, then fry each portion in an oiled pan for a crisp bottom, like the traditional stone bowl-crisped rice.

In a medium bowl, combine the cucumber, rice vinegar, sugar, and salt; stir to mix.

In a large sauté pan, heat 1 teaspoon of the oil and add the shiitakes. Sauté, stirring, until the mushrooms soften, about 4 minutes. Add the mirin, 2 teaspoons

Continued . . .

of the tamari, and 1 teaspoon of the rice vinegar and cook until dry. Transfer to a bowl and keep warm.

In the same pan, pour the remaining teaspoon of oil and add the spinach—this should deglaze the pan and remove any sauce that was sticking to the pan. Add the black garlic and stir until the spinach starts to wilt, then add the remaining teaspoons tamari and rice vinegar. Stir until softened.

If using tofu, you can either warm it or use at room temperature. If using eggs, fry them to desired doneness in a large sauté pan.

Serve a cup of rice in each bowl, topped with ¼ of the mushrooms, spinach, carrots, tofu or an egg, and a couple tablespoons of kimchi, and sprinkle with nori shreds. Serve with gochujang on the side.

# Sardine Sushi Bowl with Mango, Cucumber, and Pickled Ginger

Sardines may be an acquired taste, but they are packed with essential fatty acids. What's more, they are a relatively sustainable fish. Sardines are typically sold in cans, and this convenience is a selling point. They provide a strong flavor that complements this arrangement of sushi-esque tastes. I like to add shreds of mineral-rich nori at the end, but that's up to you.

Yield: 4 servings

4 cups cooked short-grain brown rice
1 tablespoon ume vinegar or rice vinegar
8 ounces sardines in olive oil with lemon (reserve oil)
1 medium cucumber, peeled and sliced
1 small mango, peeled, pitted, and sliced
2 cups sunflower sprouts
4 large scallions, sliced on a diagonal
¼ cup pickled ginger, sliced
Soy sauce, to taste
Wasabi, to serve
Shredded nori, if desired

Warm the rice, then fold in the ume vinegar.

Serve ¼ of the rice in each bowl, then arrange the sardines, cucumber, mango, sprouts, and scallions over the rice. Tuck the pickled ginger in between the other toppings.

If desired, drizzle with some reserved lemon oil from the sardine can. Drizzle with soy sauce, serve a dollop of wasabi, and sprinkle the nori on each bowl.

# Japanese Soba Bowl with Hemp-Coated Tofu, Slaw, Ginger, Greens, and Wasabi Cream

Oh, soba, you own a piece of my heart. The slippery, nutty-tasting soba noodle fills a bowl with healthy comfort. It is perfect as a base for greens, cabbage, pickled ginger, and amazingly delicious hemp-crusted tofu sticks. Make this bowl for folks who think they don't like tofu—these tasty bites have won over skeptics!

Yield: 4 servings

Canola oil, for pan
1 (14-ounce) package firm tofu, drained
1 large egg
1 tablespoon water
¾ cup hemp seeds
½ teaspoon kosher salt
2 tablespoons fresh orange zest
1 teaspoon red pepper flakes
6 tablespoons mayonnaise
1½ teaspoons wasabi paste
2 teaspoons rice vinegar
2 cups shredded cabbage
4 cups braising greens, coarsely chopped
¼ cup sliced pickled ginger
8 ounces soba noodles

Preheat the oven to 400°F. Lightly oil a sheet pan. Drain the tofu, wrap in a towel, and press gently to remove excess water. Slice the block lengthwise into ½-inch slices, then stack the slices and slice again, lengthwise, into ½-inch-wide strips.

In a medium bowl, whisk the egg with the water. In a large bowl, mix the hemp seeds, kosher salt, orange zest, and red pepper flakes.

Dip each tofu slice into the egg, then the hemp seed mixture, then place on the sheet pan, leaving 1 inch of space between them. Bake for 25 minutes, until crisped and browned.

While the tofu bakes, mix the mayo, wasabi, and rice vinegar in a medium bowl. Reserve 2 tablespoons of the dressing for the soba and mix the remaining with the cabbage in a medium bowl.

In a steamer, quickly steam the greens, drain, and mix with the pickled ginger in a bowl.

Cook the soba according to package instructions, drain, and toss with the reserved mayo dressing and divide between four bowls. Top each bowl equally with the cabbage slaw, greens, and tofu strips.

# Freekeh-Sage Bowl with Turkey, Celery, Green Beans, and Walnuts

Looking forward to Thanksgiving? This bowl has the flavors of your favorite stuffing and turkey, piled up with nutty freekeh and green beans. Sage provides a deep, herby complement to the earthy tastes of many grains, so there's no reason to save sage for November. This bowl is super easy to make if you use smoked turkey from the deli. Vegetarians can substitute a favorite non-turkey alternative.

Yield: 4 servings

2 cups water
1 cup freekeh
½ teaspoon dried thyme
1 pinch salt
2 tablespoons extra-virgin olive oil, divided
12 ounces green beans, stems removed
1 medium carrot, thinly sliced
2 ribs celery, chopped
2 tablespoons fresh sage, chopped
12 ounces sliced or shredded smoked turkey
¼ cup chopped walnuts, toasted

Bring the water to a boil in a 1-quart saucepan with a tight-fitting lid. Add the freekeh, thyme, and salt and return to a boil, then cover and reduce the heat to low. Cook for 25–30 minutes, until the water is completely absorbed. Stir in a teaspoon of the olive oil.

In a large sauté pan, heat the remaining olive oil over medium-high heat, then add the green beans and carrots, and stir. Stir until the green beans are lightly browned and shriveled, about 5 minutes. Add the celery and sage and stir for a minute more.

Portion ¼ of the cooked freekeh into four bowls, then divide the green bean mixture between the bowls. Divide the turkey between the bowls and top with chopped walnuts. Serve warm.

# Greek Bulgur with Spinach, Pickled Beets, Orange, and Feta

Spinach and feta are a time-tested match, carrying Greek salads and spanakopita for as long as there have been sheep to milk and greens to pick. Build a bowl using these Mediterranean standbys, and enjoy the spinach–feta combo in a liaison with sweet and tart beets, oranges, and a sprinkling of tender pine nuts.

Yield: 4 servings

**4 cups cooked bulgur**
**4 ounces salad spinach, chopped**
**2 ounces feta cheese, drained, divided**
**2 tablespoons balsamic vinegar**
**2 tablespoons extra-virgin olive oil**
**½ teaspoon dried oregano**
**3 large oranges, divided**
**1 cup pickled beets, sliced**
**¼ cup toasted pine nuts**

Heat up the cooked bulgur. Stir the spinach into the hot bulgur and put the lid back on, letting it steam for about 5 minutes to wilt the spinach.

While the spinach wilts, make the dressing. Crumble 2 tablespoons of the feta into a 2-cup measure or medium bowl. Stir in the balsamic vinegar, olive oil, and oregano, and squeeze in the juice of half of one of the oranges.

Peel the remaining oranges, then slice across each orange to make rounds, and pop out any seeds.

To serve, divide the bulgur between four bowls and drizzle half the dressing over it; stir quickly with a fork. Cover the bowls with orange slices, beets, and remaining feta, then drizzle with the remaining dressing and sprinkle with pine nuts.

# Indonesian Noodle Bowl with Boiled Eggs and Creamy Cashew Dressing

Look to Indonesia for intensely flavorful, light foods that satisfy. For this bowl, raw cashews are puréed to make a creamy, spicy sauce that adds weight to a mound of crisp veggies and tender noodles. Boiled eggs, or tofu, up the protein content. And, instead of noodles, you can always build this bowl on a foundation of cooked rice or grains instead.

Yield: 4 servings

8 ounces whole-wheat fettucine or rice noodles
½ cup chopped shallot, divided
2 cloves garlic, peeled
½ teaspoon red pepper flakes
1 cup raw cashews, plus more for garnish
3 tablespoons soy sauce
2 tablespoons light brown sugar, packed
2 tablespoons fresh lemon juice
6 tablespoons water
1 large cucumber, peeled and chopped
2 cups grape tomatoes, halved
½ cup fresh mint
4 large eggs, boiled, peeled, halved
Toasted cashews, for garnish

Cook the pasta according to package directions, then drain well. While the pasta is cooking, make the sauce. In a blender, combine 3 tablespoons of the shallots, the garlic, red pepper flakes, cashews, soy sauce, light brown sugar, lemon juice, and water. Process until smooth. Transfer to a bowl or pouring cup.

Put the pasta back in the pan and drizzle with ¼ cup of the sauce.

Divide the pasta between four bowls, then top with cucumbers, tomatoes, and mint. Arrange the halved eggs on top of the noodles. Drizzle the bowls with the remaining sauce, to taste, and top with toasted cashews. Serve warm.

# Pizza Bowl with Soft Polenta, Spinach, and Mozzarella

Pizza may be the most popular food in the world. This bowl has the familiar melty cheese, tomato sauce, and basil of pizza, all on a bowl of grainy polenta. Hearty, coarse polenta has a gorgeous yellow hue, and forms a comforting base for the pizza toppings. For a variation you could use multigrain polenta (for recipe see Multigrain Polenta with Pesto Eggs and Kale, page 38).

Yield: 4 servings

1 cup polenta
3 cups water
½ teaspoon salt
½ cup shredded Parmesan cheese
4 ounces baby spinach
1 cup prepared spaghetti sauce, heated
8 ounces fresh mozzarella, small balls or chopped
½ cup fresh basil, finely sliced

In a 2-quart saucepan, whisk the polenta, water, and salt. Place over medium-high heat, stirring, until the mixture comes to a boil. Reduce the heat to low and stir every 5 minutes, scraping the bottom of the pan to keep the polenta from sticking. Cook for 25 minutes, until the polenta is thick. Stir in the Parmesan cheese until melted. Keep warm, or transfer into a 9-inch pie pan, smooth the top, and let cool. To serve the cold polenta, reheat in the microwave or cut in wedges and sauté in olive oil until crisped and heated through.

To serve, divide the spinach between four bowls and top with the hot polenta. Measure ¼ cup of hot spaghetti sauce over each bowl and top with mozzarella. The mozzarella should soften in the hot sauce. Top with shredded basil and serve.

Alternatively, put all the ingredients into the bowls cold, and then microwave each for three minutes.

# Dinner Bowls

# Big Buddha Bowl

This bowl is big, and it brings together textures, colors, and flavors that practically add up to a main and three side dishes. The creamy golden dressing is a nutritional bonanza, with seeds and dates and turmeric puréed to a pourable elixir. The bowl will give you a different experience in every bite, and all the macrobiotic glow you look for in a bowl.

Yield: 4 servings

2 tablespoons pumpkin seeds
1 clove garlic, peeled
1 tablespoon fresh turmeric, peeled and chopped
1 tablespoon fresh ginger, peeled and chopped
2 large dates
½ teaspoon salt
2 tablespoons cider vinegar
3 tablespoons flax or hemp oil
¼ cup kombucha or water
4 cups cooked freekeh or brown rice
4 ounces kale, shredded
1 medium avocado, sliced
1 cup red cabbage, shredded
1 medium yellow beet, cubed
2 cups edamame
1 cup microgreens or pea shoots
Black sesame seeds, for garnish
Hot sauce, to serve

To make the dressing, in a food processor, combine the pumpkin seeds, garlic, turmeric, ginger, dates, and salt. Process to mince finely and scrape down, then purée to a smooth paste. With the machine running, drizzle in the vinegar, scrape down, then drizzle in the oil and kombucha. Scrape the dressing into a small pitcher or bowl.

Warm the grain and toss with 2 tablespoons of the dressing. Spread one cup on each wide bowl.

Top each bowl with kale, avocado, red cabbage, yellow beets, and edamame. Drizzle with the dressing. Garnish with microgreens, sprinkle with black sesame seeds, and serve with hot sauce on the side.

# Grits with Spicy Collards, Shrimp, Roasted Red Peppers, and Aioli Drizzle

Yield: 4 servings

**3 cups water**
**1 cup grits**
**½ teaspoon salt, divided**
**½ cup mayonnaise**
**1 clove garlic, pressed**
**1 tablespoon fresh lemon juice**
**2 teaspoons extra-virgin olive oil, divided**
**1 bunch collard greens, stems removed, sliced**
**1 teaspoon water**
**½ teaspoon red pepper flakes**
**1 pound shrimp, peeled and deveined**
**2 medium roasted red peppers, drained and sliced**

Down South, you are more likely to eat grits for breakfast than oatmeal. These chunks of dried corn are kissing cousins to polenta, and you can easily substitute polenta in this recipe. But if you can get some true, artisan grits, give them a try. Grits are sweet, creamy, and have a corny flavor that has made them a favorite. Collards, shrimp, and red peppers also grace the Southern table, so add them to this bowl and have a ball, y'all.

Bring the water to a boil in a 1-quart pot over high heat. Stir in the grits and half of the salt and cook for 5 minutes, stirring. Take off the heat, cover, and let stand for 5 minutes to thicken (or follow package directions).

While the grits cook, stir together the mayo, garlic, and lemon juice in a small bowl. Set aside.

In a large sauté pan, heat half the olive oil over medium-high heat and add the collard greens. Stir to wilt, then sprinkle in 1 teaspoon water; cover the pan for 2 minutes to soften.

Scrape the greens into another bowl and use the same pan to sauté the shrimp. Add the remaining olive oil to the pan and heat over medium-high heat. Add the red pepper flakes, shrimp, sprinkle with the remaining salt, and stir until the shrimp are pink, lightly browned, and cooked through, about 3 minutes depending on size.

Serve ¼ of the grits in each bowl. Divide the shrimp between the bowls, place the greens beside the shrimp, garnish with red pepper slices, and drizzle with mayonnaise mixture. Serve warm.

# Native Wild Rice Bowl with Dried Blueberries, Smoked Whitefish, and Sunflower Seeds

I live in Minnesota, where Native American tribes still hand harvest the best wild rice in the world. The indigenous peoples of the Upper Midwest lived happily on the foods of the region for centuries, and I put a few of them together for this beautiful bowl. Always splurge on real, hand-harvested wild rice when you can—it is a true treat. Smoked fish, dried blueberries, and sunflower seeds top the rice to create a hearty, truly American bowl.

Yield: 4 servings

4 cups cooked wild rice
2 tablespoons canola oil, divided
8 ounces shiitake mushrooms, or other wild mushrooms
2 small yellow squash, quartered and sliced
¾ teaspoon salt, divided
2 tablespoons maple syrup
1 tablespoon cider vinegar
4 cups dandelion greens or arugula, chopped
½ cup toasted sunflower seeds
½ cup dried blueberries
8 ounces smoked whitefish, crumbled
16 edible flowers, such as nasturtiums or calendulas

Warm the cooked rice.

Preheat the oven to 400°F. Spread 1 tablespoon of the canola oil on a sheet pan and put the shiitakes and yellow squash slices on the oil, sprinkle with ¼ teaspoon salt, and toss to coat. Roast the vegetables for 15 minutes, then stir and roast for 10 minutes more to soften and brown slightly.

In a small cup, stir the remaining canola oil with ½ teaspoon salt, maple syrup, and cider vinegar. Drizzle half into the wild rice and toss to mix.

In four wide bowls, spread the greens, then top with wild rice, sunflower seeds, blueberries, and whitefish. Garnish with flowers.

# Three Sisters Bowl

The original, indigenous inhabitants of North America were skilled gardeners. They developed a companion planting system called the "Three Sisters" in which corn stalks served as supports for climbing bean vines, and squash plants sprawled in between to cover the ground so that no weeds could grow. This combination of foods (corn, beans, and squash) is bigger than the sum of its parts, imparting complete proteins and complementary nutrients that sustained the Native peoples for centuries. This recipe is a modern version of this tradition. Sweet corn, butternut squash, and kidney beans are topped with a cranberry dressing, and set upon a choice between the quinoa of South America and the wild rice of the Upper Midwest.

Yield: 4 servings

4 cups cooked wild rice or quinoa
¾ cup dried cranberries, divided
1½ pounds butternut squash (4 cups cubed)
1 tablespoon butter
3 tablespoons fresh thyme
¼ cup water
2 tablespoons cider vinegar
3 tablespoons honey
½ teaspoon salt
½ teaspoon freshly ground black pepper
6 tablespoons canola oil
1 cup corn kernels
2 cups cooked kidney beans, drained

Warm the wild rice or quinoa. Boil a cup of water and take off the heat, place ½ cup of the dried cranberries in a heat-safe cup, and pour the boiling water over to cover. Let the cranberries soften while you prepare the squash.

Halve, seed, and peel the squash, slice into 1- to 2-inch-wide pieces, then cut into cubes. In a large sauté pan, heat the butter over medium-high heat and add the squash and thyme. Sauté, tossing, until the cubes start to brown. Add the water, cover, and reduce the heat to medium for 5 minutes. Uncover and test by piercing with a paring knife. When the squash is tender, leave uncovered to cook off the liquids. Take off the heat.

To make the dressing, drain the soaked cranberries. In a food processor, process the cranberries until finely minced. Add the vinegar, honey, salt, and pepper and process, scraping down and repeating until it is smoothly puréed. Add the canola oil and process until well-blended and smooth.

Measure ¼ cup of the dressing and stir into the cooked grain. Divide the grain between four bowls. Top with the squash, corn kernels, and kidney beans. Drizzle with the remaining dressing

# Cellophane Noodles, Charred Broccolini and Cauliflower, Purple Kraut, and Creamy Hemp Dressing

Have you tried charring your veggies? Believe it or not, a little burnt edge gives the brassicas a tinge of pleasant bitterness, as the high heat concentrates their flavors to the essence. Tangy fuchsia-colored kraut and creamy hemp dressing balance the intense flavors of the charred vegetables. Don't skimp on the dressing; it provides the protein in the meal.

Yield: 4 servings

1 cup slivered red cabbage
1¼ cups sauerkraut, divided
Canola oil, for pan
2 cups broccolini, cut in large florets
2 cups cauliflower
¾ cup hemp seeds, divided
2 tablespoons ginger, peeled and chopped
¾ cup apple juice
2 tablespoons toasted sesame oil
2 tablespoons tamari soy sauce
12 ounces cellophane noodles, or other noodles

Put on a large pot of water to cook the noodles. Preheat the oven to 425°F.

Meanwhile, in a medium bowl, combine the red cabbage and 1 cup of the kraut, and mix vigorously; give it a squeeze or two to really knead the kraut into the cabbage. Let stand until ready to use or for up to two days.

Lightly oil a sheet pan with canola oil and spread the broccolini on one half and cauliflower on the other half. Roast for 20 minutes, until the vegetables are blackened and softened. Take out and let cool.

In a blender or food processor, combine ½ cup of the hemp seeds, the remaining ¼ cup kraut, and the ginger; process to mince. Add the apple juice, sesame oil, and tamari and process until smooth. Scrape out into a small bowl.

Cook the noodles according to package instructions; divide between four bowls. Divide the cabbage mixture and cauliflower and broccoli between the bowls, then drizzle with the hemp dressing. Sprinkle with remaining hemp seeds and serve.

# Sweet Potato "Rice" with Barbecued Chicken or Tofu, Sweet Corn, Coleslaw, and Blue Corn Chips

Sweet potato "rice" stands in for grains here, adding a touch of sweetness and bright color. This one is a medley of picnic sensations, with barbecued chicken, corn from the cob, and slaw all in one place. You don't have to wait for summer to have a bowl that, in a few bites of bliss, takes you to a treasured summer memory.

Yield: 4 servings

**4 cups Sweet Potato "Rice" (page 8)**
**2 teaspoons canola oil, divided**
**1 (14-ounce) package firm tofu, cubed, or 1 pound chicken breast, cubed**
**1 tablespoon tamari soy sauce**
**6 tablespoons barbecue sauce, divided**
**2 cups shredded cabbage**
**½ cup shredded carrots**
**¼ cup mayonnaise**
**1 tablespoon honey**
**1 tablespoon Dijon mustard**
**¼ teaspoon salt**
**1 cup corn kernels, canned or frozen, drained**
**16 blue corn tortilla chips**

Make the Sweet Potato "Rice" and keep warm.

Preheat the oven to 400°F. Spread 1 teaspoon of the canola oil on a sheet pan and set aside.

Toss the tofu or chicken in a large bowl with remaining canola oil, tamari, and 2 tablespoons barbecue sauce. Bake the tofu for 15 minutes, then use a spatula to turn the pieces and bake for 15 minutes more. Chicken will take 10 minutes per side.

To make the slaw, mix the shredded cabbage and carrots with mayonnaise, honey, Dijon, and salt.

Portion a cup of sweet potato "rice" in each bowl, top with tofu, slaw, and corn kernels. Drizzle with remaining barbecue sauce. Garnish with chips and serve.

# Soft Polenta with Roasted Smoky Chickpeas, Grape Tomatoes, Chard, and Creamy Basil Sauce

More magic from smoke! Smoked paprika gives familiar chickpeas a sexy, summery kiss of flavor. The soft, creamy polenta is purely comforting, and it cradles the chard and tomatoes like an Italian nonna's bosom.

Yield: 4 servings

1½ cups medium-grind cornmeal
1 teaspoon salt, divided
3 cups water
1 cup milk
1 tablespoon butter
½ cup shredded Parmesan cheese
3 tablespoons extra-virgin olive oil, divided
1½ cups cooked chickpeas, rinsed and drained
½ teaspoon smoked paprika
1 cup fresh basil
1 clove garlic
2 ounces chèvre (goat cheese)
½ cup plain yogurt (not Greek)
1 large bunch chard, washed, stemmed and dried
1 cup grape tomatoes, halved

In a 2-quart saucepan, combine the cornmeal and ½ teaspoon salt, then gradually whisk in the water and milk. Over medium heat, whisk while it comes to a boil. Reduce heat to keep it just bubbling, and scrape the bottom of the pan as you stir every 5 minutes for about 20 to 30 minutes. When it reaches the desired thickness, stir in Parmesan. Keep warm.

In a large sauté pan, heat 1 tablespoon of the olive oil over medium-high heat. Add the drained chickpeas and shake in the pan, rolling them around until they start to pop and crackle. Cook for about 5 minutes,

Continued . . .

until slightly browned. Sprinkle with smoked paprika and ¼ teaspoon salt, then transfer to a bowl.

In a food processor, mince the basil and garlic. Add the chèvre and yogurt and 1 tablespoon of olive oil and process until smooth.

In the large sauté pan, heat the remaining tablespoon of olive oil and sauté the chard until wilted and dark green, and add remaining ¼ teaspoon salt.

Serve ¼ of the polenta in each bowl, topped with ¼ of the chard and chickpeas, ¼ of the grape tomatoes, and drizzled with 3 tablespoons of basil sauce per bowl.

# Teriyaki Salmon and Red Rice Bowl with Sweet Miso Dressing

Beautiful, glazed salmon is arrayed on a bed of mahogany rice that is studded with bright scarlet beets and laced with green sprouts. Crunchy wasabi peas add a spicy kick, as you savor the subtle flavors of red miso and ginger over all of it. This bowl would also be gorgeous with black rice or even multicolored quinoa.

Yield: 4 servings

8 ounces salmon fillet
Oil, for pan
1 tablespoon honey
2 teaspoons tamari soy sauce
1 tablespoon ginger, peeled and minced
4 cups cooked red rice
½ cup red miso
½ cup honey
¼ cup ginger, peeled and minced
½ cup apple juice
¼ cup canola oil
1 cup pickled beets
2 cups sunflower or pea sprouts
1 cup wasabi peas

Preheat the oven to 400°F. Cut the salmon in 4 even portions, then place the salmon on an oiled sheet pan. Stir the honey, tamari, and ginger together and spread over the salmon. Bake for about 15 minutes; test by piercing with a paring knife to see if the center is cooked. Let cool.

Warm the rice.

For the dressing, stir together the miso, ½ cup honey, and ginger to make a paste, then stir in the apple juice and canola oil.

On four wide pasta bowls, spread ¼ of the rice, then arrange the salmon, beets, sprouts, and wasabi peas. Drizzle with dressing and serve warm.

# Okonomiyaki Scramble-Topped Rice with Tomato and Mayo Drizzles

Okonomiyaki is a traditional Japanese omelet in which all sorts of tasty tidbits are cooked in a matrix of egg, then drizzled with mayo and ketchup sauces. Here, a bowl of rice anchors a simple egg scramble with all the other flavors of this omelet, so you can get a taste of Japan in your bowl.

Yield: 4 servings

**4 cups cooked short-grain brown rice**
**2 tablespoons tomato paste**
**2 teaspoons tamari soy sauce**
**½ teaspoon Dijon mustard**
**1 tablespoon mirin**
**¼ cup mayonnaise**
**2 teaspoons wasabi paste**
**1 teaspoon canola oil**
**4 cups cabbage, thinly sliced**
**1 cup carrots, thinly sliced**
**½ cup chopped onion**
**6 large eggs**
**1 teaspoon salt**
**1 teaspoon sugar**

Warm the rice and reserve until time to serve.

In a small bowl, mix the tomato paste, tamari, Dijon mustard, and mirin and set aside. In another bowl, mix the mayonnaise and wasabi paste and reserve.

In a large sauté pan, smear the canola oil and place over medium-high heat. Add the cabbage, carrots, and onion and sauté, stirring, until the cabbage is softened and carrots are crisp-tender. In a medium bowl, whisk the eggs, salt, and sugar, then pour over the veggies in the pan. Scramble until the eggs are cooked.

Serve ¼ of the rice in each bowl, with the egg scramble on top. Drizzle each with the tomato and mayo sauces and serve.

# Brown Rice and Kidney Bean Bowl with Corn, Pickled Red Onions, and Queso

This easy, fast bowl is a lively pile of Mexican-American ingredients, all sparked by a quick pickle of red onions. Pick your heat level when you select your salsa. You can choose little-kid mild or go all the way to chili-head hot—it is up to you.

Yield: 4 servings

4 cups cooked brown rice or quinoa
½ medium red onion, thinly sliced to make 1 cup
¼ cup apple cider vinegar
2 tablespoons sugar
¼ teaspoon salt
1½ cups cooked kidney beans, drained and rinsed
1 cup frozen corn, thawed
4 cups salad spinach, chopped
1 cup salsa
4 ounces queso fresco, chopped

Warm the grain and reserve until time to serve.

Place the sliced onions in a medium bowl and add the vinegar, sugar, and salt. Toss to mix thoroughly, then let stand for at least 30 minutes to soften. The onions will shrink down to about half the original volume.

Heat the beans and corn separately, if desired.

To serve, place ¼ of the chopped spinach in each bowl, then cover with grain. Top with beans, corn, and pickled onions; drizzle with salsa and cover with cheese. Serve hot.

Can also be assembled, leaving the pickled onions off, microwaved until hot, then topped with onions.

# Spaghetti Caesar with Kale, Peppers, Anchovies, Peas, and Parmesan

Have you noticed that Caesar salads are everywhere? That's because the combination of garlic, lemon, olive oil, and anchovies, with a dusting of Parmesan, makes everybody happy. Here, this combination is bathing some hearty whole-wheat pasta, kale, and peas. If you are not so into the anchovies, you can leave them out ... but perhaps you should give them a try. Just a touch of them gives the dish a meaty mouthfeel you can only get from a fermented protein.

Yield: 4 servings

¼ cup mayonnaise
1 clove garlic, minced
1 tablespoon extra-virgin olive oil
1 tablespoon fresh lemon juice
½ teaspoon freshly ground black pepper
17 whole anchovies, divided, to taste
½ teaspoon salt, none if using anchovies
8 ounces roasted red peppers, drained and slivered
8 ounces kale, stems removed, chopped
8 ounces whole-wheat angel hair, water salted
½ cup frozen peas
½ cup shredded Parmesan cheese, divided

Put on a pot of water to boil for the pasta, and salt it generously.

In a small bowl, combine the mayo, garlic, olive oil, lemon juice, black pepper, and two anchovies (if using) or salt, and mash and stir to combine. Reserve.

Drain and sliver the roasted red peppers. Warm the roasted peppers by dunking in the boiling water or microwaving.

Blanch the kale in the water for the pasta, scooping it out after 2 minutes with a spider or slotted spoon. Drain well, then pat dry with a towel. Cook the pasta with the peas according to package directions, about 4 minutes. Drain well.

Put the pasta and peas back into the pot and add 2 tablespoons of the mayo mixture and half the Parmesan cheese, and toss to coat. Divide between four bowls, and top each with ¼ of the kale and peppers, and drizzle with the remaining dressing. Top with remaining cheese and anchovies, if desired.

# Sesame Noodles with Thai Green Curry Tofu, Red Cabbage, and Snap Peas

Coconut milk is the magic ingredient in this bowl; it makes a sauce in one quick step. Just heat the coconut milk with some curry paste and a few other ingredients, and suddenly you have a rich, complex feast of Thai essential tastes. Whole-wheat linguine, or any noodle, is fantastic when coated with this lush sauce and topped with crunchy vegetables.

Yield: 4 servings

1 (14-ounce) package firm tofu
¾ cup coconut milk (half a 14.5-ounce can)
1 tablespoon green curry paste
2 teaspoons fish sauce
1 tablespoon brown sugar
8 ounces snap peas, trimmed
1 large carrot, julienned
8 ounces whole-wheat linguine
1 tablespoon toasted sesame oil
2 cups red cabbage, shredded
Slivered scallions, for garnish

Put on a pot of water to cook the pasta. Meanwhile, drain the tofu and wrap in a towel, then place a cutting board on top to remove excess water, for about 20 minutes.

Cube the tofu in ¾-inch pieces and reserve. In a large sauté pan, combine the coconut milk and green curry and mash with a spatula to combine. Place over medium heat and bring to a simmer; stir in the fish sauce and brown sugar. Add the tofu and carefully turn to coat. Let simmer, stirring and turning occasionally, for about 5 minutes, until the coconut milk is thick.

In the boiling water (before the pasta goes in), poach the snap peas for just a minute, then scoop out with a slotted spoon and reserve. Poach the carrots for about a minute, scoop and reserve. Cook the linguine according to package directions, about 4 minutes, and drain well. Transfer to a bowl and toss with sesame oil to coat.

In each of four bowls, portion the cooked linguine, then top with snap peas, carrots, red cabbage, and the tofu and sauce from the pan. Garnish with scallions and serve hot.

# Roasted Vegetable Bowl with Hazelnut Gremolata

When Brussels sprouts and sweet potatoes are roasted, it concentrates their sweet, intense flavors. You can even caramelize the edges for maximum appeal. All that deep earthiness is perfectly lifted up with a chop of parsley, garlic, lemon, and hazelnuts. Barley or any hefty grain is a perfect base for this medley of yum.

Yield: 4 servings

3 tablespoons extra-virgin olive oil, divided
1 pound sweet potatoes, cut into ½-inch cubes
1 pound Brussels sprout, halved
1 large shallot, slivered
4 cups cooked pearled barley or other grain
1 cup fresh parsley
1 clove garlic, peeled
2 teaspoons fresh lemon zest
½ cup toasted and skinned hazelnuts
¾ teaspoon salt

Preheat the oven to 425°F. Spread 1 tablespoon of the olive oil on a sheet pan.

Place the sweet potato cubes, Brussels sprouts, and shallot in the oil and toss to coat. Roast for 25 minutes, then stir and check for doneness by piercing with a paring knife. When the sweet potatoes are tender and the Brussels sprouts are browned, take out and let cool slightly.

Warm the barley and keep warm.

On a cutting board, mince the parsley, garlic, and lemon zest until fine, then add the hazelnuts to the pile and chop them coarsely. Transfer the parsley mixture to a medium bowl and stir in the remaining 2 tablespoons olive oil and the salt.

Serve 1 cup cooked barley in each bowl, covered with ¼ of the roasted vegetables, then sprinkle with ¼ of the parsley mixture. Serve immediately.

# Brown Rice Taco Bowl with Ground Beef or Mushroom Sauté, Shredded Vegetables, Green Salsa, and Jack Cheese

Ditch the packages of fried taco shells and build your tacos on a bowl of rice. It's also so easy to sub minced mushrooms for ground beef—just sauté the succulent mushroom bits until dark and concentrated. Fresh shredded veggies and green salsa work magic with the pepper jack cheese.

Yield: 4 servings

4 cups cooked brown rice or quinoa
1 cup shredded cabbage
1 cup shredded carrots
1 tablespoon fresh lime juice
½ teaspoon salt
2 teaspoons canola oil
1 cup chopped onion
12 ounces ground beef or button mushrooms
1 teaspoon chili powder
1 teaspoon oregano
4 ounces pepper jack cheese, shredded
½ cup green salsa (salsa verde)

Cook or warm the grain. In a medium bowl, combine the cabbage, carrot, lime juice, and ¼ teaspoon salt; toss to coat.

In a large sauté pan, heat oil and add the onion; cook for about 5 minutes to soften. Add the ground beef, breaking it up as it cooks, and sprinkle with the chili powder, oregano, and remaining salt. Cook over medium-high heat until the beef is browned and cooked through, about 5 minutes. (For the mushroom version, use a processor to mince the mushrooms finely, then add to the pan instead of ground beef. Proceed, cooking until the pan is dry.)

Serve 1 cup cooked rice in each bowl, topped with beef or mushrooms, ¼ of the shredded vegetables and the jack, and 2 tablespoons of salsa.

# Fish Taco Bowl with Soft Grits, Cabbage, Lime Chili-Baked Fish, and Tomatoes

Mexican and Southern foods have formed a fusion of their own, and grits are a perfect player in that game. Instead of tortillas, soft and creamy grits say Georgia, while the fish taco fixin's say SoCal. We can dig in wherever we live, just because this bowl is so dang tasty.

Yield: 4 servings

1 cup grits
2 cups water
1 cup whole milk
½ teaspoon salt
Canola oil, for pan
1 pound salmon or other firm fish
1 teaspoon ancho chile powder
1 teaspoon oregano
2 teaspoons light brown sugar
1 teaspoon coarse salt
3 cups shredded red and green cabbage
½ cup sour cream or crema
1 teaspoon fresh lime zest
1 tablespoon fresh lime juice
1 cup cherry tomatoes, sliced
¼ cup cilantro, torn
½ cup pickled red onions, optional (from Brown Rice and Kidney Bean Bowl with Corn, Pickled Red Onions, and Queso recipe, page 96)
Hot sauce, optional

Preheat the oven to 400°F.

In a 1-quart pot, combine the cooked grits, water, milk, and salt and place over high heat to bring to a boil. Stir frequently. Once it boils, turn to low and cover; stir

Continued . . .

every 5 minutes for a total of 15 minutes. It should be thick. Take off the heat and let stand, covered.

Use canola oil to smear on a sheet pan for the salmon. Slice the fish into four portions and place on the pan, not touching. In a cup, mix the chile powder, oregano, light brown sugar, and salt. Sprinkle over the salmon pieces and pat to adhere. Bake the salmon for 10 to 15 minutes, just until pink in the center.

In a medium bowl, mix the cabbage, sour cream or crema, lime zest and juice.

In each bowl, serve 1 cup of grits, topped with ¼ of the fish, ¾ cup of the cabbage salad, ¼ cup cherry tomatoes, and a tablespoon of cilantro. Add pickled red onions and hot sauce if desired.

# Bulgur Asparagus Radish Bowl with Kombucha Green Goddess Dressing

This is a spring bowl, perfect for displaying your best local asparagus and radishes when they come to market. Adding a shot of kombucha to the dressing imbues the creamy avocado drizzle with probiotics, as well as a little tangy, fermented flavor. Crunchy green edamame is the easy protein champ, and it looks gorgeous in this pastel-themed composition.

Yield: 4 servings

1 cup cooked bulgur
¼ cup chopped fresh parsley
1 clove garlic, peeled
1 large avocado
3 tablespoons plain kombucha, or more as needed
½ teaspoon salt
4 large red radishes or 1 watermelon radish, thinly sliced
1 bunch asparagus, steamed
1 cup edamame, shelled, thawed

Cook or warm the bulgur and keep warm. Stir in parsley.

In a food processor, mince the garlic clove, then scrape down and add the avocado. Process until smooth. Add the kombucha and salt and process to mix well, adding a little more as needed to make a pourable dressing.

Arrange ¼ of the bulgur in each bowl; top with radishes, asparagus, and edamame. Drizzle with the dressing.

# Black Rice with Chickpeas, Cucumbers, Peppers, Tomatoes, and Tzatziki Sauce

Tzatziki sauce is a gift from the gods, if you believe in such things. Just a bit of dill and some cucumber gives yogurt full standing as a Greek sauce, with no effort at all. You can make extra for drizzling on other dishes, or even pile extra on this bowl. Protein and probiotics team up to give your topper healthy benefits, and the simple combination of black rice, chickpeas, and veggies suddenly comes together as a fine meal.

Yield: 4 servings

4 cups cooked black rice
1 large cucumber, divided
1 clove garlic, pressed
1½ cups plain yogurt (not Greek)
1 tablespoon fresh dill, more for garnish
½ teaspoon salt
2 cups cooked chickpeas, drained
1 cup cherry tomato, halved
2 medium roasted red peppers (jarred), drained, patted dry, sliced
Dill sprigs, for garnish

Warm the rice.

To make the tzatziki, peel the cucumber, then use a spoon to scoop out the seeds. Grate half the cucumber into a medium bowl and reserve the other half. To the medium bowl, add the garlic, yogurt, dill, and salt. Stir to mix. Slice the remaining half cucumber into half-moons.

To assemble the bowls, portion a cup of cooked rice, then ½ cup of chickpeas, ¼ of the tomatoes, red peppers, and sliced cucumbers. Dollop ½ cup of tzatziki sauce on top of each bowl and serve, garnished with dill sprigs.

# Brothy Bowls

# Quick Pho Broth-Poached Shrimp and Vegetables over Rice

Quick, say "pho!" If it rhymed with "go," you are saying it American-style. The correct pronunciation is "fuh." You will thank me the next time you visit your local Vietnamese restaurant and roll out your pho order. In the meantime, this lively version is an easy, excellent stand-in. Hefty whole grains are a good alternative to rice starch noodles, and the lively Vietnamese broth is infused with dried mushrooms and star anise. Pile on fresh cilantro, scallions, and jalapeño, and then squeeze a lime wedge over it and you are golden.

Yield: 4 servings

4 cups cooked brown rice, quinoa, or barley
1 quart vegetable stock
1 tablespoon fresh ginger, peeled and chopped
4 large dried shiitake mushrooms
1 star anise
½ medium cinnamon stick
1 tablespoon tamari soy sauce
1 tablespoon brown sugar
1 pound shrimp, shelled and deveined
1 large carrot, sliced thinly on a diagonal
4 ounces snap peas, trimmed
4 medium scallions, diagonally sliced
½ cup cilantro leaves, whole
1 small jalapeño, sliced
1 large lime, quartered

Warm the grain and set aside.

To make broth, pour the vegetable stock into a 2-quart pot, and add the ginger, dried mushrooms, star anise, and cinnamon stick. Bring to a boil and reduce to a simmer, covering the pot while you prepare the rest of the ingredients. Let it simmer for at least 15 minutes, then season with tamari and brown sugar.

Portion the cooked grain into four bowls and reserve. Drop the shrimp into the simmering stock and cook until pink and completely cooked through, about 3 minutes, depending on the size. Use a skimmer to scoop out the shrimp and arrange them on top of the cooked grain. Add the carrot to the pot and boil for 1 minute, then add the peas and cook for 1 minute more.

Ladle the hot broth over the bowls, about one cup per bowl.

Top the bowls with scallion, cilantro, and jalapeño. Squeeze a lime wedge on top and serve immediately.

# Cure a Cold Brothy Bowl

Bookmark this one for that inevitable day when you feel a sniffle coming on. Cook up a batch of immune-boosting, throat-soothing soup, and share it with anyone you may have already gifted with your germs. It's a beautiful thing when something tastes this good and also supports your healing magic.

Yield: 4 servings

1 quart vegetable stock
4 slices fresh ginger, peeled, thinly sliced, then slivered
4 slices fresh turmeric, peeled, thinly sliced, then slivered
2 large garlic cloves, crushed
1 large lime, divided
1 large jalapeño, slivered
1 large carrot, chopped
1 tablespoon tamari soy sauce, plus 2 tablespoons for baking
1 tablespoon canola oil, for pan
1 (14-ounce) package firm tofu, drained and cubed, or ¾ pound cooked chicken
4 ounces fresh spinach, chopped
4 cups cooked brown rice, freekeh, or other grain
Red pickled ginger, for garnish
Scallions, diagonally sliced, for garnish
Microgreens, for garnish

Preheat the oven to 400°F.

In a 4-quart pot, bring the vegetable stock to a boil, then reduce to a gentle simmer. Add the ginger, turmeric, garlic, ¼ of the lime, jalapeño, carrot, and tamari. Cover and simmer on low or medium-low heat to gently infuse the stock.

On a sheet pan, smear the canola oil, then pile the tofu cubes on it. Sprinkle with tamari and then spread on the pan. Roast for 30 minutes. For chicken, cut or tear into bite-sized pieces.

In each of four bowls, place ¼ of the spinach, then a cup of cooked grain. Top with ¼ of the tofu cubes or chicken, then ladle the broth on top.

Garnish with red pickled ginger, scallions, and microgreens.

# Lemongrass-Poached Scallops and Veggie Brothy Bowl over Whole-Wheat Noodles

Lemongrass, garlic, and ginger give this broth a Southeast Asian jolt, and jalapeños kick it up just a bit more. Once the broth is fully infused, the whole bowl of veggies, noodles, and tender scallops will have a kiss of citrus. Use asparagus in spring, and use more seasonal veggies the rest of the year, like zucchini in summer and parsnips in winter.

Yield: 4 servings

1 quart vegetable or chicken stock
1 large lemongrass, split lengthwise and bruised with the back of a knife
1 tablespoon ginger, peeled and chopped
2 cloves garlic, chopped
1 tablespoon fish sauce
8 ounces whole-wheat spaghetti or grain of choice
1 large jalapeño
4 medium carrots, chopped
1 bunch asparagus, tough bottoms removed
1 pound small scallops, trimmed
Black sesame, for garnish
½ cup fresh cilantro, torn

Put on a large pot of water to cook the spaghetti. Meanwhile, in a 4-quart pot, combine the stock, lemongrass, ginger, garlic, and fish sauce and bring to a boil. Cover and reduce the heat to low to simmer while you cook the rest of the bowl. Simmer for at least 30 minutes.

Boil the spaghetti and drain. Divide the cooked noodles between four bowls. Uncover the simmering stock, stir in the jalapeños. Push the lemongrass to one side, then poach the carrots for about 2 minutes, scooping them out with a slotted spoon and distributing between the bowls. Poach the asparagus for about a minute, and divide

Continued . . .

between the bowls. Poach the scallops, just until the edges crack a little and the flesh is white. Cut one in half at 2 minutes to see if it is just a little translucent in the center and white all around that. Scoop out and divide between the bowls.

Use tongs to remove the lemongrass and discard, then divide the stock mixture between the bowls. Top with black sesame on the scallops and cilantro over the rest.

# Chipotle Lime Brothy Bowl with Chicken over Quinoa

Smoky chipotles are a bonanza for cooks in a hurry. Simply open a can of smoked chipotle in adobo sauce; mince one and freeze the rest. Toss the minced chipotle and a chunk of lime into some boxed stock, and simmer it while you prep the rest of the ingredients. The pervasive smoky heat will infuse into the broth and make a bowl of quinoa, vegetables, and chicken or tofu into a powerfully tasty meal.

Yield: 4 servings

4 cups chicken or vegetable stock
1 medium canned chipotle pepper in adobo sauce, minced
2 cloves garlic, sliced
1 medium lime, divided
½ teaspoon salt
2 large carrots, chopped
1 medium zucchini, quartered and sliced
4 cups cooked quinoa
1 pound cooked chicken breast or mock duck, bite-sized
½ tablespoon finely chopped red onion
½ cup cilantro leaves, torn
Sour cream, for garnish, optional

In a 4-quart pot, combine the stock, chipotle pepper, garlic, half the lime (squeeze the lime and then drop it into the pot), and salt. Cover the pot and bring to a boil, then reduce the heat for 10 minutes to build the flavor.

Add the carrots and zucchini and simmer for 5 more minutes, just to soften the carrots and zucchini. Taste for heat, add more adobo sauce if it seems mild to you. Smash the lime against the side of the pot with a spoon and remove the spent peel.

In each bowl, arrange 1 cup cooked quinoa, ¼ of the cooked chicken, and ladle the stock and vegetables in each bowl. Garnish with red onion and cilantro, and a dollop of sour cream, if desired.

# Hot and Sour Tofu and Sweet Potatoes over Rice Noodles

Drop by your local Chinese restaurant and you will surely find a hot and sour soup on the menu. Unfortunately, it will probably be loaded with MSG and enough sodium to elevate even the healthiest person's blood pressure. Luckily, the broth for a hot and sour soup is easy enough to make more healthfully at home. Simply ladle it over the noodles and veggies, all crowned with tofu.

Yield: 4 servings

4 cups vegetable or chicken stock
1 tablespoon rice vinegar
1 teaspoon sugar
1 tablespoon tamari soy sauce
½ teaspoon coarsely cracked black pepper
2 cups cubed sweet potato (12 ounces before trimming)
8 ounces black rice ramen or other noodle
1 (14-ounce) package firm tofu, drained and cubed
1 cup shredded red cabbage
2 large scallions, diagonally sliced

In a 4-quart pot, bring the stock to a simmer over medium heat. Add the vinegar, sugar, tamari, and pepper. Add the cubed sweet potatoes to the pot and cover. Simmer for 5 minutes, then uncover and test a cube by piercing with a paring knife. When the sweet potatoes are tender, remove them to a bowl with a slotted spoon.

Add the noodles to the pan and stir, cooking until they are tender, gently separating them as you stir, about 4 minutes.

Divide the noodles between four bowls. Top them with ¼ of the tofu, sweet potatoes, and cabbage, and then pour the warm stock over them all. Top with scallions and serve immediately.

# Miso-Poached Vegetable and Shrimp Millet Bowl

Miso poaching is an old Japanese technique. By cooking each ingredient in a miso and sweet mirin broth, you cook everything just enough, all while making the miso broth more concentrated with each poach. By the time you get to the shrimp, you will have a savory stock worthy of saucing your big, fluffy bowl of millet.

Yield: 4 servings

**2 cups water**
**2 tablespoons mirin**
**2 tablespoons red miso**
**8 ounces broccoli**
**8 ounces cauliflower**
**2 large carrots, sliced**
**1 pound shrimp, peeled and deveined**
**4 cups cooked millet**
**4 sheets seasoned nori**

In a wide skillet or soup pot, combine the water, mirin, and miso; whisk to mix, and bring to a boil over medium-high heat. Add the broccoli and poach for about 2 minutes; use a skimmer or slotted spoon to remove the broccoli to a plate. Poach the cauliflower for about 3 minutes, remove, and poach the carrots for 2 minutes and remove.

After poaching the veggies, add the shrimp and cover the pot (if the pan is getting dry, add more water).

Cook until the shrimp is pink and completely cooked, about 3 minutes depending on the size.

Serve 1 cup millet in each of four bowls, and arrange equally the vegetables and shrimp on top. Pour the remaining miso broth over the bowls. Sprinkle with nori. Serve warm.

Big Party
Platter Bowls

# Black Rice Bánh Mì Bowl with Quick Pickled Veggies and Five-Spice Seitan or Chicken

Yup, bánh mì is the super-popular sandwich that melds French bread with Vietnamese fillings, all slathered with mayo. In this fabulous platter, the tender rice gets a drizzle of sriracha-infused mayo, and the sweet-and-sour pickled daikon and carrots pile on top with five-spice chicken (or mock duck.) This bowl has all the things you love in a proper bánh mì, spread out on gorgeous black rice that makes for a striking presentation.

Yield: 8 servings

4 ounces daikon, shredded
1 large carrot, shredded
¼ cup rice vinegar
1 tablespoon sugar
½ cup mayonnaise
2 tablespoons rice vinegar
1 tablespoon sriracha sauce
2 medium cucumbers, peeled and sliced
2 large jalapeños, sliced
4 large scallions, slivered
1 tablespoon canola oil
1½ pounds chicken or mock duck, chopped
1 teaspoon five-spice powder
1 tablespoon fish sauce or tamari soy sauce
6 cups cooked black rice
1 cup cilantro leaves, whole

In a medium bowl, combine the daikon, carrots, rice vinegar, and sugar and toss to mix. Let marinate for at least 30 minutes, or overnight. In a small bowl stir the mayonnaise, rice vinegar, and sriracha sauce; reserve.

Slice the cucumbers, jalapeños, and scallions and reserve.

Heat a large sauté pan over medium-high heat, then drizzle with canola oil, swirl to coat. Add the chicken

Continued . . .

or mock duck and sprinkle with five-spice and stir. As the chicken sears, it will release from the pan, so give it a couple of minutes before turning. When the chicken or mock duck is almost cooked through, pour the fish sauce over it and stir and toss until the pan is dry and all the chicken is coated. Take off the heat.

On a large platter, spread the cooked rice, then drizzle with the mayo sauce. Compose the daikon mixture, cooked chicken, sliced vegetables, and cilantro leaves. Serve.

# Farro with Artichokes, Roasted Peppers, Feta, and Balsamic Drizzle

This big party bowl will make you want to drop all your fussy appetizers, store your potato salad recipe, and start collecting cool platters. Spread out a bunch of uber-popular farro, top with easy-to-prep veggies (canned artichokes and peppers score!), and sprinkle with feta and a tasty dressing. Let your friends and family scoop it up, while you party with the best of them.

Yield: 8 servings

5 tablespoons extra-virgin olive oil, divided
1 large fennel bulb
4 large garlic clove, peeled
2 tablespoons balsamic vinegar
1 teaspoon salt
1 teaspoon Dijon mustard
1 teaspoon cracked black pepper
6 cups cooked farro
4 ounces arugula or spinach leaves, washed and dried
1 (15-ounce) can artichoke bottoms, drained and patted dry, cut into 6ths
1 (8-ounce) jar roasted peppers, drained and patted dry, slivered
4 ounces feta cheese, crumbled

Preheat the oven to 400°F. On a sheet pan, spread 1 tablespoon of the olive oil.

Trim the fennel bulb, saving the greens. Slice the bulb and the base of the stems into ½-inch cubes and place on the sheet pan. Scatter the pan with the garlic cloves. Toss to coat. Cover the pan with foil and roast the fennel and garlic for 20 minutes. Uncover the pan and roast for 15 minutes longer, until the garlic is tender when pierced with a paring knife. Let cool.

In a cup, combine the balsamic vinegar, salt, Dijon mustard, and pepper and whisk. Whisk in the remaining 4 tablespoons of olive oil. Place the cooked farro in a large bowl, pour half the dressing over the farro, and toss to mix.

On a large platter (about 16 inches round) spread the arugula. Pile the farro on the greens, then arrange the artichoke pieces, roasted peppers, fennel, and feta, then drizzle the remaining dressing over it all.

# Paleo Cauliflower Tabouli Deluxe with Peppers, Carrots, Cashews, and Lemon-Mint Dressing

We all know and love tabouli. Even so, it is really overdue for a makeover. Carb avoiders have been using cauliflower bits to replace grains, and in a dish like this it really works. Bright, lemony, minty dressing makes cauliflower exciting, and the piles of herbs and vegetables are a healthy side we can all get behind. Serve this and watch it disappear!

Yield: 8 servings

2 pounds cauliflower
2 cups fresh mint, minced, plus sprigs for garnish
2 cloves garlic, peeled
1 teaspoon salt
½ cup fresh lemon juice
2 tablespoons fresh lemon zest
½ cup extra-virgin olive oil
2 large cucumbers, peeled, seeded, and sliced
2 large carrots, shredded
2 medium tomatoes, chopped
1 large green pepper, seeded and chopped
1 cup roasted cashews, coarsely chopped

Put on a large pot of water to boil for the cauliflower. Cut the cauliflower into large florets and peel the stems; cut the stems into 1-inch slices. When the water boils, drop in the cauliflower. Cook for 2 minutes, then drain. Let the cauliflower cool, then put 2 cups of florets in a food processor and pulse to make bits about the size of rice.

Transfer to a large bowl, then continue until all the cauliflower is minced. Spread a lint-free kitchen towel on the counter and spread the cauliflower mince on it; place another towel on top and roll up tightly to dry. Unroll the towels, remove the top one, and let the cauliflower air dry until time to use.

In a food processor or blender, process the mint, garlic, and salt to a mince. Add the lemon juice, zest, and olive oil and process until the mint is finely puréed. Transfer the cauliflower to a large bowl and drizzle half of the lemon-and-olive-oil mixture over the cauliflower, tossing to coat.

Spread the cauliflower on a platter, then cover with cucumbers, carrots, tomatoes, peppers, and cashews. Drizzle with the remaining dressing. Garnish with mint sprigs.

# Sweet Potato "Rice" with Roasted Tofu, Boiled Eggs, Chayote, and Gado Gado Peanut Sauce

I love this combination of flavors so much: the sweet potatoes and creamy peanut sauce make an addictive combination, and all the textures and tastes of the vegetables just add to the fun. This lively platter is just as good with brown rice.

Yield: 8 servings

1 (14-ounce) package firm tofu
2 tablespoons tamari soy sauce
2 tablespoons dark sesame oil
2 tablespoons honey
Oil, for pan
8 cups Sweet Potato "Rice" (for recipe, see page 8) or 3 cups cooked brown rice or other grain
1 tablespoon canola oil
1 teaspoon red pepper flakes, to taste
2 large garlic cloves, minced
5 small shallots, minced
1½ cups coconut milk
6 tablespoons creamy peanut butter
1 tablespoon fish sauce
1 tablespoon sugar
1 tablespoon tamarind pulp or lemon juice
4 ounces pea tendrils, washed and dried
8 ounces green beans, blanched
2 medium chayote fruit, boiled and cooled
1 large cucumber, peeled, seeded, and sliced
6 large eggs, hard boiled, peeled, and halved lengthwise
1 cup Thai basil, shredded

Drain the tofu and wrap in a kitchen towel to blot dry. Slice the tofu into slabs about ¾-inch thick. In a flat-bottomed storage container that is large enough to hold the tofu, whisk the tamari, sesame oil, and honey. Place each tofu slice in the marinade, turning to coat. Cover and refrigerate overnight, flipping the container upside down a couple of times to coat evenly.

Preheat the oven to 425°F and lightly oil a sheet pan. Place the marinated tofu on the pan, and roast for 20 minutes, then turn the slices and roast for 20 minutes more. Cool on a rack.

Heat the sweet potato "rice" or brown rice and let cool.

To make the sauce, in a 2-quart pot, heat the canola oil over medium-high heat. Add the pepper flakes, garlic, and shallots and stir. Reduce the heat to low and sauté the shallots until clear and soft, about 4 minutes. In a medium bowl, stir the coconut milk and peanut butter to make a smooth paste. Stir into the shallots in the pan. Add the fish sauce, sugar, and tamarind and stir. Bring to a boil over medium heat, stirring. The sauce will thicken slightly.

Drizzle a third of the sauce over the Sweet Potato "Rice" and toss to coat.

Spread the sweet potatoes on a large platter. Arrange the pea tendrils, green beans, chayote, cucumber, and tofu on top. Place the boiled and halved eggs around the platter. Drizzle with sauce and garnish with Thai basil. Serve.

# Southwestern Quinoa with Avocados, Black Beans, Shredded Cabbage, Jalapeños, and Crema-Cilantro Drizzle

Everybody loves a burrito, right? This big, festive bowl is packed with all the spicy, limey excellence that makes burritos such crowd pleasers. Kids and adults will pile their bowls high with healthy quinoa and beans, all the while thinking it's just party food.

Yield: 8 servings

6 cups cooked quinoa
2 cloves garlic, peeled
3 large jalapeños, seeded
1 cup cilantro leaves, whole, plus more for garnish
1 teaspoon lime zest
1½ cups Mexican crema or sour cream
1 teaspoon salt
3 cups black beans, cooked, rinsed, and drained
3 cups shredded cabbage
2 large tomatoes, chopped
3 large ripe avocados

Warm the quinoa.

In a food processor or blender, mince the garlic, 1 jalapeño, and cilantro leaves. Scrape down, then add the lime zest, crema, and salt. Process until smooth.

Spread the quinoa on a large platter, then arrange the beans. Sliver the remaining 2 jalapeños and arrange them and the cabbage, tomatoes, and avocados on top. Drizzle with the cilantro mixture and serve.

# Mediterranean Party Bowl

Get in on the freekeh trend, and pair it with the classic Mediterranean flavors it was meant to accompany. This spread of lemony basil-strewn grain is covered with an entertaining assortment of sweet, sour, savory, and salty delights. Soft dates melt in your mouth between bites of briny olives and sweet roasted peppers. The tuna is optional—the platter is fantastic either way.

Yield: 8 servings

6 cups cooked freekeh
1½ cups fresh basil, divided
2 cloves garlic, peeled
½ cup fresh lemon juice
½ cup extra-virgin olive oil
¼ cup honey
1 teaspoon salt
4 ounces salad spinach
6 ounces soft, pitted dates, torn in strips
1 cup oil-cured or kalamata olives, halved
½ cup capers, drained
2 large roasted red peppers, drained, patted dry, and slivered
4 cans tuna in oil, optional

Warm the freekeh. In a food processor or blender, process 1 cup of the basil with the garlic to a mince. Add the lemon juice and olive oil and process until well combined, then add the honey and salt and process to mix. Drizzle half the basil mixture on the freekeh and toss to mix.

On a large platter, spread the spinach, then cover with the freekeh. Arrange the dates, olives, capers, and red peppers on the freekeh. If desired, drain the tuna, break into chunks, and pile in the center of the freekeh. Drizzle with the remaining dressing. Sliver the remaining basil and sprinkle over the platter.

Dessert Bowls

# Sweet Purple Rice with Pineapple and Crushed Cashews

In Thailand and many other tropical countries, desserts are less about butter and cream and more about a little sweetness and fruit. Nobody wants to bake in that tropical heat, much less try to move after eating a bunch of cake. Lush rice-based treats like this one are the norm, with richness coming from the coconut and a refreshing topping of sweet pineapple.

Yield: 4 servings

1½ cups water
1 cup Thai purple sticky rice
1½ cups coconut milk, divided
1 pinch salt
¼ cup palm sugar or brown sugar
1 (3-pound) pineapple, peeled and chopped (4 cups)
½ cup roasted, unsalted cashews, crushed
1 medium lime, for zest curls

Bring the water, rice, coconut milk, and salt to a boil in a 1-quart saucepan with a lid. Once it boils, reduce the heat to low, cover, and cook for 35–40 minutes, until all the water is absorbed. Let stand, covered.

Heat the remaining coconut milk with the palm sugar just to dissolve the sugar.

Mix half of the coconut milk mixture into the pineapple, then divide it between the bowls. Drizzle with the remaining coconut sauce and top with cashews and lime zest curls.

Note: To make lime zest curls, use a channel knife and pull it across the peel of the lime. If you don't have a channel knife, use a peeler to remove long strips of zest and then slice them thinly.

# Honey-Cinnamon Drizzled Farro with Strawberries, Cocoa-Chèvre, and Walnuts

Chocoholics, rejoice! This bowl is topped with disks of deep, chocolatey chèvre that are ready to melt into the warm, honey-drizzled rice. If you have had a light dinner and are still hungry, this will top you off, guaranteed. Crunchy walnuts finish the bowl, making this an altogether grown-up affair.

Yield: 4 servings

3 cups cooked farro
8 ounces chèvre, softened
2 ounces bittersweet chocolate, melted
¼ cup cocoa
2 tablespoons powdered sugar
¼ cup plain Greek yogurt
½ teaspoon vanilla
¼ cup honey
1 teaspoon cinnamon
8 large strawberries, hulled and sliced
1 cup walnut pieces

Warm the farro.

In a medium bowl, mash the chèvre, then quickly mix in the melted chocolate. Mash in the cocoa, powdered sugar, Greek yogurt, and vanilla. Stir until well mixed. Place an 8-inch piece of plastic wrap on the counter and form the chèvre into a 1-inch-thick rope; wrap in plastic and chill.

In a cup, stir the honey and cinnamon.

To serve, place ¾ cup warm farro into each bowl and top with slices of chèvre, strawberries, walnuts, and the honey-cinnamon drizzled over it all.

# Creamy Pistachio Oats with Cherries and Shaved Chocolate

Oats for dessert? You bet! The same creamy sweetness that we love about oats at breakfast makes for a lush, pudding-like bowl at the end of the meal. Pistachios, puréed with honey and a touch of cream, give the oats a slightly exotic vibe, as well as a greenish tint. Add sweet Bing cherries and a few shreds of chocolate, and you will wonder why you never made oats for dessert before!

Yield: 4 servings

10 ounces frozen Bing cherries
1 tablespoon sugar
¼ teaspoon almond extract
½ cup shelled pistachios
2 tablespoons honey
¼ cup cream
3 cups cooked steel-cut or whole oats
1 ounce dark chocolate

In a 1-quart pot, warm the cherries, add the sugar and almond extract and bring to a boil. Cook until the juices are slightly thickened, about 5 minutes.

In a food processor, grind the pistachios to a fine powder. Add the honey and cream and process until smooth.

Warm the oats.

In the pot, stir the pistachio mixture into the oats. Divide the oat mixture between each of four bowls. Top with ¼ of the cherries and juice, then use a swivel peeler to shave chocolate over each bowl. Serve warm.

# Banana Pudding and Red Rice Trifle

A trifle is one of those old-timey desserts, like a syllabub or an icebox cake, and it deserves an update. Here, sweet and nutty red rice is layered with a real egg yolk–infused custard. And the whole thing is studded with bananas and then topped with whipped cream. Nobody would call this spa food, and that is okay.

2 cups whole milk
4 large egg yolks
½ cup granulated sugar
¼ cup unbleached flour
¼ teaspoon salt
2 tablespoons butter
1 teaspoon vanilla
3 cups cooked red rice
¼ cup maple syrup
1 teaspoon almond extract
2 medium bananas
¼ cup whipping cream
1 tablespoon powdered sugar
½ teaspoon vanilla

To scald the milk, put the milk into a 1-quart pan and place over medium-high heat. Bring just to a boil and take off the heat; let cool completely.

In a medium bowl, whisk the egg yolks until they are pale and thick. In a 2-quart pot, whisk the sugar, flour, and salt. Gradually whisk in the cooled milk. Whisk a little of the milk mixture into the egg yolks, then whisk the yolks into the milk mixture in the pan.

Place the pan over medium heat and whisk constantly until the mixture comes to a boil; whisk constantly as you let it bubble for a few seconds, then take off the heat and whisk in the butter and vanilla.

Continued . . .

Transfer to a bowl and cover with plastic wrap, pressing the plastic onto the surface of the pudding so it won't form a skin. Chill completely.

Warm the red rice. Mix the maple syrup and almond extract into the rice and let cool.

To assemble, slice ⅙ of a banana into each of four glass bowls. Top with ¼ cup rice mixture, and dollop ¼ cup of the pudding on top, spreading it gently to cover.

Top with another ⅙ of a banana, ½ cup of rice, and ½ cup of custard, spreading it gently to the edges.

In a small jar, combine the whipping cream, powdered sugar, and vanilla, and screw the lid on tightly. Shake the jar vigorously for a few minutes, until the cream thickens. (You can also whip the cream with an electric mixer in a large bowl.) Spoon the whipped cream onto the parfaits and garnish with remaining banana.

# Maple-Almond Oat Bowl with Chocolate Chips and Mango

Fat, creamy oat groats are just as appropriate for a dessert as the rolled kind. Really, they are. Break out of your usual dessert habits and try this easy, nutty sweet treat. It's as easy as stirring up a little sauce and sprinkling on a few irresistible toppers.

Yield: 4 servings

**4 cups cooked whole-oat groats**
**¼ cup almond butter**
**¼ cup maple syrup**
**1 teaspoon cinnamon**
**1 teaspoon almond extract**
**1 cup honey roasted almonds, coarsely chopped**
**2 large mangos, peeled and sliced**
**¼ cup miniature chocolate chips**

Warm the oats.

In a medium bowl, stir the almond butter, maple syrup, cinnamon, and almond extract. Add the warm oats and stir to coat the grains with the almond butter mixture.

Portion the oats into four bowls and top with chopped almonds, mango slices, and chocolate chips on top. Serve warm.

# Creamy Oats with Strawberries and Lemony Cheesecake Sauce

Cheesecake may have seen its day as a hot fad, but we all still love the taste of cream cheese filling. Why not lift it out of that tired old crust and make it into a leaner, more lemony drizzle for your oats and berries? If a cup of yogurt can claim to taste like chocolate truffles, then this bowl can promise to ring your cheesecake bells.

Yield: 4 servings

6 ounces Neufchatel cheese, softened
1½ teaspoons fresh lemon zest, plus more for garnish
1 tablespoon fresh lemon juice
3 tablespoons honey
½ cup plain yogurt (not Greek)
½ teaspoon vanilla
4 cups cooked steel-cut or whole-oat groats
1 pound fresh strawberries, washed, dried, and sliced

In a food processor, process the Neufchatel cheese until completely smooth, scraping down and repeating until there are no lumps. Add the zest, juice, honey, yogurt, and vanilla and process until smooth. Scrape into a 2-cup liquid measuring cup for easy pouring. If you plan to refrigerate the sauce, stir in a couple of tablespoons milk so it will not get too thick to pour.

Warm the oats.

To serve, portion ¼ of the oats into each of four bowls, top with the cheesecake sauce, and arrange strawberries on top. Sprinkle with a little lemon zest for color and serve.

# Cocoa Brown Rice Bowl with Berries and Peaches, Topped with Streusel Crunch

A little cocoa and some creamy cheese melt into the hot brown rice, instantly dessertifying the healthy whole grains. Fresh fruit tossed with honey and orange juice positively bursts with sunshine, and the crunchy streusel topper is too tasty to be denied.

Yield: 4 servings

2 ounces Neufchatel cheese or chèvre
2 tablespoons cocoa
2 tablespoons brown sugar
½ teaspoon vanilla
4 tablespoons milk, approximately
4 cups cooked brown rice blend
2 tablespoons freshly squeezed orange juice
2 tablespoons honey
2 6-ounce packages blackberries or raspberries, washed and dried
2 large peaches or plums, pitted and sliced
½ cup streusel, (see Nutty Cinnamon Streusel Granola Topper, page 20)
Orange zest strips, for garnish

Warm the rice.

In a medium bowl, mash the cheese until creamy. Add the cocoa and brown sugar and mash and mix into a paste. Add the vanilla and stir in the milk a tablespoon at a time until it makes a creamy mixture. Stir into the warm rice.

In another bowl, mix the orange juice and honey, then add the berries and peaches and toss to coat.

Serve a cup of rice in each bowl, topped with fruit mixture, and then streusel. Garnish with orange zest. Serve warm.

# Buttermilk Quinoa Bowl with Praline Pecans

I won't try to deceive you—making pralines is a bit of a production. The first time you make them, they might not be perfect. But once you master the simple art of boiling the sugar and pecans to the right temperature, you will be glad you did. A classic Southern candy, the praline is both smooth and crunchy, and it makes great use of the local pecans. Peaches and buttermilk round out the Southern profile, giving exotic quinoa a down-home feel!

Yield: 4 servings

¾ cup granulated sugar
6 tablespoons light brown sugar
¼ cup 2% milk
3 tablespoons unsalted butter
½ teaspoon vanilla
1 cup pecan halves
4 cups cooked quinoa
1 cup buttermilk
1 cup Greek yogurt
¼ cup sorghum syrup or honey
10 ounces frozen sliced peaches, thawed

First, make the pralines. Spread a piece of waxed paper on a sheet pan.

In a 4-quart pot, mix the granulated and brown sugars, milk, butter, vanilla, and pecans. Over medium-high heat, bring to a boil. Once boiling, stir constantly for about 2 minutes, until the mixture reaches 240°F on a candy thermometer. Take off the heat immediately and keep stirring; stir and beat until the mixture thickens and becomes lighter colored. When it just starts to get grainy, quickly spoon the mixture into tablespoon-size portions onto the waxed paper, leaving room in between.

Let the pralines harden at room temperature. Store in an airtight container for a couple of days.

Warm the quinoa. Whisk the buttermilk, Greek yogurt, and sorghum in a cup, then stir into the warm grain. Serve topped with peaches and pralines.

# Chocolate Buckwheat with Pistachios, Dried Cherries, and Whipped Cream

Chocolate and buckwheat go together: The bitter sweetness of chocolate makes the natural sweetness of the buckwheat more prominent. The fat, tender grains are a toothsome carrier for a gloss of melty chocolate and a crunchy flourish of pistachios. Tart and tangy dried cherries pull it all together, and a creamy updo of whipped cream is a fitting finish. You can swirl some full-fat Greek yogurt on top, if you want to be a little less decadent.

Yield: 4 servings

3 cups cooked buckwheat groats
¼ cup mini-chocolate chips
½ cup dried cherries
½ cup roasted pistachios, chopped
½ cup whipped cream or vanilla Greek yogurt

Warm the buckwheat. Stir in the chocolate to melt. Cover and let stand until serving.

In each bowl, portion the buckwheat, ring the bowl with cherries, sprinkle with pistachios, and dollop whipped cream or Greek yogurt in the center.

# Acknowledgments

This book and just about everything I do is made possible by the unwavering emotional support of Stanley Asbell, my partner in love, life, and most dinners.

Thanks to my editors Ann Treistman and Sarah Bennett, and to my amazing agent, Angela Miller. It takes a team to bring a book into the world.

The beauty of this book is due to the talents of photographer David Schmit and food stylist Bret Bannon, who worked with me to create the images that grace these pages. I can't say enough about how talented, professional, and fun these guys are.

Thank you to Seton Rossini for the beautiful design. Thanks to the Countryman production team, Devon Zahn and Natalie Eilbert, and to Devorah Backman, Countryman's publicist.

I'd also like to thank Erik Riese, who generously loaned me his gorgeous handmade bowls for several of the photos, including: Three Sisters Bowl (page 84), Lemongrass-Poached Scallops and Veggie Brothy Bowl over Whole-Wheat Noodles (page 119), Indonesian Noodle Bowl with Boiled Egg and Creamy Cashew Dressing (page 72), Cure a Cold Brothy Bowl (page 116), Quick Pho Broth-Poached Shrimp and Vegetables over Rice (page 115), Buckwheat and Seared Cabbage with Braised Squash Chunks and Smoked Almonds (page 61), and Multigrain Polenta with Pesto Eggs and Kale (page 38). Check him out on Etsy: www.etsy.com/people/santaerik.

Eternal thanks to my father, Larry Calhoun, for creating the handmade platters and bowls that appear in the photos for Black Rice Bánh Mì Bowl with Quick Pickled Veggies and Five-Spice Seitan or Chicken (page 128), Paleo Cauliflower Tabouli Deluxe with Peppers, Carrots, Cashews, and Lemon-Mint Dressing (page 133), Soft Polenta with Roasted Smoky Chickpeas, Grape Tomatoes, Chard, and Creamy Basil Sauce (page 91). I owe him so much.

Profuse thanks to my recipe testers, Melodie Bahan, Lisa Genis, and Kristine Vick, who were kind enough to try the recipes out and serve them to their family members. The feedback was invaluable.

Bob's Red Mill generously provided some fantastic grains for our recipe testing, and I can vouch that they are a brand that can be counted on for top-quality grains for all your bowls.

# Index